THE EIGHT PRAYER WATCHES

The Secret Power To Command, Control
And Transform Your Life

Book Layout by .....

First Edition.
ISBN 978-0-6921042-3-1
Printed in the United States of America

THE EIGHT PRAYER WATCHES

The Secret Power To Command, Control
And Transform Your Life

"But keep alert at all times [be attentive and ready], praying that you may have the strength and ability [to be found worthy and] to escape all these things that are going to take place, and to stand in the presence of the Son of Man [at His coming]."

(Luke 21:36 AMP)

Ebenezer B. Gyasi

The Eight Prayer Watches
The Secret Power To Command, Control And Transform Your Life

Deliverance-On-The-Go-Ministries
23 Colgate Dr.
Newark, NJ. 07103
www.dotgomin@yahoo.com

CONTENTS

DIVINE DEDICATION

Yes
And
Amen!

Glory be to God, Abba Father!

Whose fatherly love always and forever embraces and sustains us
and has given us the victory through Christ Jesus, His Son.

Glory be to the Lamb of God!
To His Son Jesus Christ our Master and Savior,
who has given us authority, power, and victory
over the Kingdom of Darkness.

Glory be to the Spirit!
To the Holy Spirit—the One who teaches us
how to war and our fingers to do battle-

The Teacher, and the Revealer of
prophetic hidden truths and mysteries and by
whose wisdom and power, the contents of this
Battle of the Kingdoms prayer points
were assembled, to equip the Saints
for effective deliverance ministry
to advance God's Kingdom on earth

Hallelujah!
And
Amen!

Do

You

Know

The Power of Night Vigil Prayers?

"Arise, and let us go by night, and let us destroy her palaces."
(Jeremiah 6:5)

"And all of them conspired together to come and attack Jerusalem
and create confusion. Nevertheless, we made our prayer to our God,
and because of them we set a watch against them day and night."
(Nehemiah 4:9-10)

PRELUDE

THE MYSTERY OF PRAYER WATCHES

THE QUESTION HAS BEEN ASKED whether we need to pray in a particular time of the day for our prayers to become more effective. To some people, whether you pray only in the morning, or in the afternoon, or in the evening, makes no difference. Really?

For example, let's assume you choose to pray only in the morning and at night, when you come under spiritual attack in the afternoon why wait 8 or 12 hours later, to react and pray? Why wait until calamity and tragedy strikes before praying to seek the face of the Lord? Why suffer pain and loss when you could have been on your guard watching onto prayer with all due diligence? Why do you think Jesus warned us to pray without ceasing?

Do you know that there are certain spiritual phenomena which occur at specific times of the day with profound consequences for your life, and the destiny of your City, State, and Nation either from God or the devil?

1

Although the enemy, our adversary targets and attacks us all the time, in Psalms 91 we read,

"You shall not be afraid of the terror by night, Nor of the arrow that flies by day, Nor of the pestilence that walks in darkness, Nor of the destruction that lays waste at noonday."

(Psalm 91:5-6 NKJV)

With this knowledge would you only invoke God's protection in the morning and not the rest of the day?

Others have said that it doesn't matter what time you pray, because all that matters to God is your heart. The time for prayer and the intentions of your heart are two different things although they are interrelated.

There is more to prayer than the good intentions of your heart. Here is a prayer secret you should know. In the realm of the spirit, good intentions, passion and emotions do not supersede the legality of an issue or to a situation. There are gates, doors, windows, and portals that open and close at specific times and appointed seasons as mandated by God in alignment with the heaven ordinances, and until you have knowledge and understanding of certain spiritual matters, your best efforts at prayer will not be enough and can lead to failures, disappointments in unanswered prayers, petitions, supplications, and intercessions and even a backlash from the kingdom of darkness. We must learn to be alert, watch, pray and tap into these treasures and blessings that have been made available to us.

As Believers, we must be active and proactive participants in the spiritual realm. Know for sure that:

2

- Each hour of the prayer watches carries a release and a call on your destiny.

- The Eight Prayer Watches together releases special revelation knowledge, assignments, guidelines, instructions, and directions for your life.

- It's up to us to earnestly seek, tap, invoke and take possession of these resources as part of your inheritance from your heavenly Father!

The truth you acquire from this book will reveal and equip you with the mystery power of prayer watches to

- alert you as to when to pray and command,
- control, and transform your life,
- the destiny of your family,
- your loved ones, and
- empower your ministry for effective results!

THE EVIL WILL BOW DOWN BEFORE THE GOOD AND THE WICKED [WILL BOW DOWN] AT THE GATES OF THE RIGHTEOUS.

(Proverbs 14:19 AMP.)

Jesus Gives a Parable about Prayer

One day Jesus taught the apostles to keep praying and never stop or lose hope. He shared with them this illustration:

[2] "In a certain town there was a civil judge, a thick-skinned and godless man who had no fear of others' opinions.

[3] And there was a poor widow in that town who kept pleading with the judge, 'Grant me justice and protect me against my oppressor!'

[4-5] "He ignored her pleas for quite some time, but she kept asking. Eventually he said to himself, '..., I'll just get her off my back by answering her claims for justice and I'll rule in her favor. Then she'll leave me alone.'"

[6] The Lord continued, "Did you hear what the ungodly judge said—that he would answer her persistent request?

[7] Don't you know that God, the true judge, will grant justice to all of his chosen ones who cry out to him night and day? He will pour out his Spirit upon them. He will not delay to answer you and give you what you ask for.

[8] God will give swift justice to those who don't give up. So be ever praying, ever expecting, just like the widow was with the judge. Yet when the Son of Man comes back, will he find this kind of persistent faithfulness in his people?"

(Luke 18:1-8 The Passion Translation – TPT)

"Be joyful in hope, patient in affliction, faithful in prayer."

(Romans 12:12 NIV)

INTRODUCTION

TRANSFORMING POWER OF PRAYER WATCHES

What is a watch? The Merriam-Webster defines a watch as "to be attentive or vigilant." A watch is a period (time and season) of watchful attention maintained at night, or at other times. The Hebrew night watch was made up of three watches; the First, the Middle and Morning Watches during the customary hours of sleep. However, under the Roman influence and dominion, it was increased to four-night watches as follows:

- 1st Watch (6:00pm-9:00pm);
- 2nd Watch (9:00pm-12MN);
- 3rd Watch (12MN-3:00am);
- 4th Watch (3:00am-6:00am).

The Eight Prayer Watches are comprised of four-night watches as listed above and four-day watches as follows:

- 5th Watch (6:00am-9:00am);

- 6th Watch (9:00am-12Noon);
- 7th Watch (12Noon-3:00pm);
- 8th Watch (3:00pm-6:00pm).

One may question the importance of observing prayers at certain times of the day and in which order we keep them. Let me ask you a question, the calamity that the enemy brings on people during the daytime, when was it hatched? Granted that you know the date of an attack, when or how do you plan to tackle, defend, and control your day before your enemies initiate their assault on you?

In view of the above scenarios, are there specific and definite strategic patterns or keys for prayers? Does it matter what, when, and how you pray? Yes! Stop beating about the bush! Nothing in the spiritual world happens by chance. Don't leave problems and solutions to chances! Seek expedient and effective ways of handling problems!

Heavenly Ordinances

There are cosmic laws which govern the activities of the universe. For example, there are cosmic powers that rule the day, and the night that God has programmed into creation as written:

"And God said, Let there be lights in the firmament of the heaven to divide the day from the night; and let them be for signs, and for seasons, and for days, and years: ... And God made two great lights; the greater light to rule the day, and the lesser light to rule the night: he made the stars also. And God set them in the firmament of the heaven to give light upon the earth, to rule over the day and over the night, and to divide the light from the darkness: and God saw that it was good."

(Genesis. 1:14-18)

The above scripture passages point to the role of the Sun and Moon and other heavenly bodies to carry out certain spiritual and physical duties and mandates. God created the heavenly bodies and itemized their duties as follows:

1. To divide the day from the night.
2. To rule day and night (See Psalm 121:6).
3. To give light upon the earth.
4. For signs.
5. For seasons.
6. For days.
7. For years.

These cosmic powers are to declare the glory of God according to Psalm 19 and not to be worshipped. However, the kingdom of darkness and their agents have harnessed these powers and have found a powerful way for carrying out their evil assignments to perpetrate wickedness, to hurt the innocent as evidenced in wrecked homes, families, finances, fragmented souls, numerous truncated destinies, and the tragic loss of many lives. Do you know how to harness these laws to your advantage? Here is how! At the beginning of Creation, God gave dominion and authority of the earth to man. In Psalm 8 it is written,

"When I see and consider Your heavens, the work of Your fingers, The moon and the stars, which You have established, What is man that You are mindful of him, And the son of [earthborn] man that You care for him? Yet You have made him a little lower than God, And You have crowned him with glory and honor. You made him to have dominion over the works of Your hands; You have put all things under his feet."

(Psalm 8:3-6AMP)

Any man who understands the dynamics of the cosmic laws of creation can become powerful and has the advantage to change the course of events on the earth either for good, or for evil! Don't allow chances to determine your destiny.

Just as our prayers attract heaven's attention, so does it attract the attention of the demonic kingdom, according to Daniel 10:12-13. The activities of the demonic in the Second heavens form barricades to block the blessings of God and answers to our prayers in the third heavens from reaching their intended recipients on earth.

Ask Daniel and he will tell you about the escapades of the Prince of Persia and his cohorts in the second heavens. But enough is enough! Power must change hands! The time of ignorance is over. Get knowledge! Get instruction!

Find, Grab And Use The Keys

Here are some key facts you may already know:

- Everything in creation was planned, designed and created for a reason and for a purpose.
- There are three heavens: The First heaven (Earth); Second heaven (for Demonic-principalities); Third Heaven (Kingdom of God).
- The spiritual realms are more powerful and rule over our natural world order.
- Humans are first spiritual and second physical.
- Therefore, human beings live on two-dimensional planes, or realms.

- The ordinances in creation affect both the spiritual and the physical realms.
- There is order in Creation with appointed seasons.
- The pattern of laws and activities in the spiritual realm does not change. As written, "While the earth remains, Seedtime and harvest, Cold and heat, Winter and summer, And day and night Shall not cease." (Genesis 8:22NKJV)
- Our God is a just and righteous Judge and He rules over all the kingdoms!

To successfully wage spiritual warfare, you need the Word of God as a tool, a weapon, and also the knowledge on how to operate and arm all areas of spiritual vulnerabilities in your life, your loved ones, and those who interact with you.

Without knowledge, His people perish according to God in Hosea 4:6. In addition, for those who do not regard the work of the LORD, nor consider the operation of His hands, and therefore lack the knowledge of God's ways, God is also lamenting and saying, in Isaiah 5:12b-14NKJV,

"My people have gone into captivity, Because they have no knowledge; Their honorable men are famished, And their multitude dried up with thirst. Therefore Sheol has enlarged itself And opened its mouth beyond measure; Their glory and their multitude and their pomp, And he who is jubilant, shall descend into it."

Therefore, know God and His Word and His ways, get spiritual knowledge, good instruction, and by faith prepare to use what you've acquired. But to maintain your victory, you must be able to stand your guard to watch and pray at all times, while pleading your case before the

Righteous and Just Judge of the Universe before engaging in spiritual warfare.

Is it any wonder the Word of God commands us to be awake, alert, to watch, and pray without ceasing? Present, plead and make your case with all manner of prayers, including supplications, petitions, and intercessions at different watches, to change the dynamics of your situation!

Here is a secret you know, to effectively deal with a problem, you must first go to the root, the source, or the foundation of that issue. Where can you find answers to the root of all human issues? In the bible! The Bible, contains the truths about all human mystery and misery as first recorded in Genesis, and ending in the book of Revelation!

It has been said that, when you pray something may happen, but when you don't pray something happens! In other words, the devil has already programmed and initiated his attack and assault into your day, it's only through prayers can you diffuse and thwart his aggressive posture towards your destiny!

Spiritually, knowing the day and what happens during your day is very important. So, the question is, when does the true day begin, or at what hour does the **new day** start? Do you know the womb of a new day? Below is some vital information to revolutionize your daily devotion and prayer life!

In the Genesis account of Creation, when God created the earth, "evening to the morning" was counted as a day. As written, "So the evening and the morning were the first day." (Day 1 Genesis 1:5, Day 2 vs. 8, Day 3 vs.13, Day 4 vs.19, Day 5 vs. 23, Day 6 vs. 31)

- Spiritually, the beginning of your new day starts at sundown, sunset, or twilight, or the evening!

- Demons, witches, and the demonic kingdom know the strategic importance of twilight or sunset. Do you?

- When you wait for sunrise or daylight to appear before praying, you are half a day or 12 hours late!

- When you come across "twilight" in mystery books, pause and think about the heavenly ordinances.

- The evening is the gateway or womb of your new day!

The evening is also the foundation of the night, and the night the foundation of daylight. Since the First Watch is the beginning of the day, whatever happens during the rest of the day (i.e. daytime) is largely impacted by what happens during the evening, and night hours. Therefore, don't forget to pray at the beginning of the watches, starting from 6 pm.

Who or what controls the gate to your day and night, to your week, month, year, and the seasons, or even the appointed times as designated by God for your destiny? It's fair to say that whoever controls the gates to the evening and night hours also controls the gates to the rest of the day, for doing business, and to interact with people either for good, or for evil.

Is it any wonder God wants us to possess the gates of our enemies? Pray for the ability to possess the enemy's gate!

Importance Of Gates

What is a gate, or door? Gates are ports of entry and exit. Technically, although a gate or door serves as an entry and exit point, it may also have the ability to function as a protective barrier, and guard against intrusion and theft. In the ancient world, the city gate was the seat of power; whoever possessed the gate of the city had the advantage. In the Bible, Nehemiah lamented about the city gate of Jerusalem being burned with fire and left in ruins. Heaven has gates, and hell, or hades (the realm of the dead) has gates!

In the realm of the spirit, gates are very important and critical to the dynamics, atmosphere and the destiny of families. Their impact on people, city, states, and nations by evil spiritual gates can be catastrophic. Therefore, possess your spiritual gates before your enemies do! In Matthew 16:18, Jesus told Peter," And I also say to you that you are Peter, and on this rock I will build My church, and the gates of Hades shall not prevail against it."

Before you possess the gates of the enemy, you must first secure your gates in righteousness. In his book, "Destiny Clinic," Dr. Olukoya lists seven major evil spiritual gates that adversely affect our destiny. Here they are:

The Gate Of Evil Altars

"Evil altars are a place of communion with demonic entities. However, with a godly altar as we find in the days of Jacob when his father, Abraham in his day had built an altar to God, Jacob saw in his dream angles ascending and descending and reasoned the place was the gate of heaven and called the place, Bethel, the house of God."

(Genesis 28:16-17)

Before many people became Christians, they may have had family altars dedicated to demons and the kingdom of darkness and therefore, instead of angels ascending and descending on those families, demonic entities would be trafficking, parading, and terrorizing, stealing, killing, and destroying people and their destinies.

Prayer Points

1. The blood of Jesus, enter into any evil altar in my foundation and destroy them in the name of Jesus.
2. You evil altar of bondage, attacking my family and my finances, break by the blood of Jesus.
3. I command all ancestral evil altars, covering my glory to catch fire, in the mighty name of Jesus.
4. I command any evil done against my destiny so far through the powers of the evil altars, be reversed by the blood of Jesus, in the name of Jesus.
5. My family and I we refuse to be caged by satanic altars, in the mighty name of Jesus of Nazareth.
6. Evil altars of spiritual attacks and death, assigned against me backfire continuously, in Jesus' name.
7. Every evil altar connecting day and night to work against me, receive fire and die, in Jesus' name.

The Gate Of Evil Covenants

Covenants, specially blood covenants are very powerful and are not easily broken. When a family head makes a covenant, it also binds and affects future generations for good or for evil. Covenants with demonic entities are binding on the family and children of subsequent generations under that covenant.

Years ago, in the Bronx, in New York, during a deliverance session, a man of God, told one gentleman that in his family house there was a door to a room that was always locked and he asked him if he knew what was behind the closed door. The man of God revealed to him that in the past, some members of his family made a covenant with a fetish, in which they were to offer human blood to the demonic god. As years passed and people became Christians, or could no longer offer human blood, they stopped appeasing the deity with the blood. But the demonic god would not be denied his sacrifice of human blood.

Therefore, every year someone from the family would die of a death that elicited blood from the victim. Anybody who marries into that family is fair game and a sacrificial lamb for the demonic god. Only by revelation and the blood of Jesus can the prayerful in the family skip and escape their turn to die prematurely be it in a car accident, gunshot wound, a knife, or bleed profusely during child birth, etc. at the hand of this god.

The Psalmist laments as follows: "If the foundations are destroyed, What can the righteous do?"

(Psalm 11:3 NKJV)

As a Christian, invoke the blood of Jesus to break the evil family covenant, and activate your blood covenant with God through the blood of Jesus Christ of Nazareth.

The Gate Of Witchcraft

In Nahum 3:4, it is written, "Because of the multitude of the whoredoms of the wellfavoured harlot, the mistress of witchcrafts, that selleth nations through her whoredoms, and families through her witchcrafts."

Witchcraft has the power to sell members of a family to other demonic entities and evil human spirits. Therefore, one single witch in a family, can sell the entire family to witchcraft. In some cultures, witchcraft is an heirloom, or an inheritance normally passed on to female members of the family and to a lesser extend to the men.

- Witchcraft, is one of the predominant ways that the enemy uses to decimate and devastate the souls and destiny of many people.
- Witchcraft is closely aligned with sexual immorality and prostitution.
- So watch and guard your sexual life carefully to avoid the fragmentation of your soul, or defile and trouble yourself with any evil soul-ties.
- Your sex organ is a very important gate to your life, and an evil enemy who possesses this gate will introduce witchcraft into your family.

Some witches also use their new-found powers to enhance themselves. Modern-day witches and wizard do not ride on brooms, or wave magic wands. They dress in fine suits, and skirts looking and smelling good, and cruising in the latest fancy cars, and they can be found all around us.

According to Dr. Olukoya, if your business is not going well, you may have had a sexual encounter with a witch and "thereby sold your family, your life, and your property and business to them."

The Gate Of Family Sins

In Exodus it is written,

"Then the Lord passed by in front of him, and proclaimed, "The Lord, the Lord God, compassionate and gracious, slow to anger, and abounding in lovingkindness and truth (faithfulness); keeping mercy and lovingkindness for thousands, forgiving iniquity and transgression and sin; but He will by no means leave the guilty unpunished, visiting (avenging) the iniquity (sin, guilt) of the fathers upon the children and the grandchildren to the third and fourth generations [that is, calling the children to account for the sins of their fathers]."

(Exodus 34: 6-7 AMP)

The sins, transgressions and inequities of our bloodline always put us into trouble with God, and with the devil. The consequence and activities of family sins follow the children and further generations. Don't let God hand you over to your enemies because of your sins, and the sins, transgressions, and iniquities of your blood line as written,

"So the anger of the Lord burned against Israel, and He gave them into the hands (power) of plunderers who robbed them; and He sold them into the hands of their surrounding enemies, so that they could no longer stand [in opposition] before their enemies. Wherever they went, the hand of the Lord was against them for evil (misfortune), as the Lord had spoken, and as the Lord had sworn to them, so that they were severely distressed."

(Judges 2:14-15 AMP)

Three other evil spiritual gates that Dr. Olukoya mentions in his book include the Gate of Negative Family Names, Curses, and Idolatry (an idol is anything that you put ahead of God, anything you love and cherish more than God, no matter who it is, or what it is!)

Here are some secrets you should know about spiritual gates:

1. In the realm of the spirit, the gatekeeper has the power, advantage to influence the dynamics of what happens to people, or a place. How?

2. That person or entity is able to dictate and change the spiritual atmosphere and physical environment over the place, or situation.

3. That person or spirit, like territorial spirits, can also supervise, control and monitor what goes in and comes out of that gate, place, or person!

4. But as a spiritual and physical being with dominion over the earth, you have authority to possess the gates of the day with your mouth.

5. As a king, and priest of the Most High God, you have the power to receive from God as a priest, and as a king makes decrees and declarations to possess gates, change the atmosphere, laws and rulings over a place, or the times, and seasons.

As stated earlier, the times and seasons have points of entry and exit and therefore have gates. Similarly, our day, our week, our month, our year, and seasons all have gates.

We must possess these gates, because if the gates of hell possess them, they must be first repossessed before the kingdom of heaven can even prevail. (Matthew. 16:18-19)

In Revelation 1:18, we see Jesus possessing the keys of [absolute control and victory over] death and of Hades (the realm of the dead).

Prayer warrior, I salute you! And as written,

"May your descendants possess the gates of those who hate them."

(Genesis 24:60 NKJV)

When you find yourself surrounded and hemmed in by the enemy's gate, it's only by strategic power-prayers can you set yourself free. But first secure your own gates before you try to possess the enemy's gate! As we talk about gates, a word of caution here is vital, especially, concerning our mouths! There are gates to almost everything, including our eyes, ears, minds, mouths, and hearts. Make sure and don't allow sin to open your gates to the enemy.

For example:

- Don't lust with your eyes.
- Don't speak
    - faithless and negative words that would
    - defile you and also,
    - energize and
    - open your gates to the enemy!
- Be Alert, Vigilant, Watch, Pray and Attack with Power and Authority through the Eight Prayer Watches!

The Power Of Prayer Watches

Since the pattern of spiritual laws and activities on the earth does not change, it can therefore be duplicated. The Eight Prayer Watches can be repeated. It's no mystery that spiritual revivals and deliverance can occur when we come together to pray as a group, or a nation.

When we pool together to pray, the multiplication power of prayer synergy is released. We find the scriptural basis for this corporate agreement in Leviticus 26:7-12 as follows:

"You will chase your enemies, and
they shall fall by the sword before you.
Five of you shall chase a hundred, and
a hundred of you shall put ten thousand to flight;
your enemies shall fall by the sword before you.
'For I will look on you favorably and
make you fruitful,
multiply you and
confirm My covenant with you.
You shall eat the old harvest, and
clear out the old because of the new.
I will set My tabernacle among you, and
My soul shall not abhor you.
I will walk among you and
be your God, and you shall be My people."

God will always come to our aid when we seek and wait on Him through watching, and praying. Our God will arise and scatter our enemies according to Psalm 68:1.

God laments about the ignorance of His people. We need spiritual teachings in order to empower our lives. Fight back by using the Eight Prayer Watches as a tool and a weapon!

Benefits Of Prayer Watches

It is reported that Pastor David Yonggi Cho's church in South Korea became a mega church after binding the strongmen over South Korea in an all-year prayer watch! Below are some benefits of prayer watches according to Susan and Fred Rowe.

1. Prayer watches invoke the love of the Lord as we obey His commands.

2. Love promotes intimacy with God.

3. Intimacy releases God's blessings. [Psalm 63:3-7; Luke 12:37]

4. Prayer watches protect defensively and help offensively in times of spiritual attack to sustain victory. [Nehemiah 4:7-9; Ezekiel 33:1-6; Jeremiah 51:12]

5. The night watches are extremely strategic and carry significant spiritual weight. [Genesis. 32:24-29; Mathew 14:24-25]

6. Prayer watches help establish righteousness and governmental order in an area or territory. [Psalm 127:1; Daniel 4:17; Isaiah 62:6-7]

7. Prayer Watches pave the way for the future. [Mark 13]

8. Through corporate agreement, the power of synergy prayer is released.

9. Combined prayer watches create a culture, and an atmosphere of prayer fellowship between and among church communities.

10. By prayer watches, we obey the command of Jesus to watch and pray and not fall into temptation.

Watch and Pray

In order to become more astute and mature spiritual intercessors, we must learn and practice how to pray 24 hours a day as a group, using tools like the eight prayer watches as a guide, with particular emphasis on the night watches because of heightened and clandestine activities of the demonic realms. The night vigils are important, because not many prayers are being offered during these hours of the day.

Hear and heed the advice of Jesus,

"But know this that if the owner of the house had known what hour the thief would come, he would have watched and not allowed his house to be broken into."

(Matthew. 24:43 NKJV)

The Church as a body must pray more often. Why? The Church cannot renegade her responsibilities to overcome evil wherever it is found.

The Church As Restrainers of Evil

The Ecclesia, the Church, as the body of Christ has been given the power to restrain evil on earth. God's governmental authority and power in the Church is further rooted in Ephesians 1:21-23 where we find that Jesus as the head of the Church is,

"Far above all principality and power and might and dominion, and every name that is named, not only in this age but also in that which is to come. And He put all things under His feet, and gave Him to be head over all things to the church, which is His body, the fullness of Him who fills all in all."

Therefore, you and I, as part of the Church, the body of Christ, we have been given the power to restrain evil on earth as written,

"For the mystery of lawlessness is already at work; only He who now restrains will do so until He is taken out of the way. And then the lawless one will be revealed whom the Lord will consume with the breath of His mouth and destroy with the brightness of His coming."

(2 Thessalonians 2:7-8NKJV)

Here on earth, God has left us in charge of His Kingdom business as written,

"To the intent that now the manifold wisdom of God might be made known by the church to the principalities and powers in the heavenly places, according to the eternal purpose which He accomplished in Christ Jesus our Lord, in whom we have boldness and access with confidence through faith in Him."

(Ephesians 3:10-12NKJV).

Besides, Jesus has given us the keys to the Kingdom of Heaven. The question is, have we been good stewards? There will be a day of accountability and so always be alert and ready for you do not know the time of the Master's return, but this is what He says to all.

"Take heed, **watch** and **pray**; for you do not know when the time is. It is like a man going to a far country, who left his house and gave **authority to his servants**, and to each his work, and commanded the **doorkeeper** to watch. Watch therefore, for you do not know when the master of the house is coming—in the **evening**, at **midnight**, at the crowing of the rooster, or in the **morning**—lest, coming suddenly, he find you **sleeping**. And what I say to you, I say to all: Watch!"

(Mark 13:33-37NKJV emphasis added)

God has given the earth to men. According to the Bible,

"The heaven, even the heavens, are the Lord's; But the earth He has given to the children of men."

(Psalm 115:16NKJV)

We must be careful not to accuse God for the suffering in Third World countries. Man is responsible for the earth to keep it pristine, fertile, and habitable for all! God's original intent and plan for mankind on earth is recorded as follows:

"God took the man and put him in the Garden of Eden to tend and keep it."

(Genesis 2:12NKJV)

Part of "keeping it" is by watching to maintain the integrity of the earth from demonic infestations and onslaughts. It is also our responsibility to keep the earth holy and not defile the land with idols and bloodshed.

God gave the earth to man with the mandate to:
1. Watch
2. Tend and
3. Keep it

We have therefore been called as:
1. Watchmen
2. Intercessors and
3. Soldiers (for defensive/offensive purposes)

In alignment with God's will concerning:
1. An issue or a problem pertaining to an individual, or a group.
2. A situation or circumstances.
3. Or a territorial region, an area, or a nation.

In a nutshell, the culture of prayer watches harnesses the presence of God and of heaven to bring transformation to:

1. Lives
2. Families
3. Communities
4. Cities
5. States
6. Nation and
7. The World

to impact our environment, situation, and destiny!

- Develop a strategy to watch and pray, day and night without ceasing or fainting as commanded by Jesus!
- Take turns and shift to pray in alignment to the word of God in Habakkuk
- Take turns and shifts to pray in alignment to the word of God in Habakkuk 2: 1 saying," I will stand upon my watch, and set me upon the tower, and will watch to see what he will say unto me, and what I shall answer when I am reproved."

In Matthew, Jesus warned His disciples,

"Watch therefore, for you do not know what hour your Lord is coming. But know this, that if the master of the house had known what hour the thief would come, he would have watched and not allowed his house to be broken into. Therefore you also be ready, for the Son of Man is coming at an hour you do not expect."

(Mat. 24:42-44 NKJV)

Prayer watches will help you to stay focused on the Lord. In the book of Isaiah, we read,

"My soul has a desire for You in the night. Yes, my spirit within me looks for You in the morning."

(Isaiah 26:9NLV)

It is written that you shall know the truth, and the truth shall set you free. However, it is the application of the truth that actually sets you free! You are in possession of this book because the Holy Spirit wants to give you the tools and weapons, knowledge, and revelation to empower you to unlock and fulfill your divine destiny! Therefore, come and let us explore the hidden power and the application of the Eight Prayer Watches!

Food For Thought

What is the chief end of prayer watches? Is your watching physical or spiritual, or both? Who has been called to watch and pray? Who has laid on your heart to watch? On whose behalf are you watching, your family, neighborhood, community, city, state, nation, or the world? What is the role of the Church with regard to watching?

Does watching involve responsibility and accountability? What do you gain by watching? Here is why we should take these prayer watches seriously.

- Everyone has been called to watch and pray! There are no exemptions!

In Romans Chapter 18, we find that,

"The creation was subjected to futility, not willingly, but because of Him who subjected it in hope; because the creation itself also will be delivered from the bondage of corruption into the glorious liberty of the children of God."

(Romans 18:20-21NKJV)

In other words, the frustrations in this world are waiting for the mature sons of God (ie: those led by the Spirit) to pray, decree, and make declarations to stop, and resist the powers of evil from destroying God's creation! Listen to what the word of the Lord in Psalm 81:6-7 is saying to you and myself, "I said, "You are gods, And all of you are children of the Most High. But you shall die like men, And fall like one of the princes." Do you want to live and die like a mere man, weak, impoverished and without power? Or would you rather live with authority and power to possess and dominate, and reign on earth according to your kingdom's mandate? The truth is before you, make your choice!

In God, there is hope for His creation, as the mature sons of God take authority to restrain the powers of evil here on earth. You can choose to live according to your divined heritage as written of you in Genesis 1:26-28, or die like a mere man, or fall like Lucifer! Again, the choice is yours, chose wisely!

The title of this book does not adequately portray the full essence of what the book is all about. This book can also be appropriately titled, "The Eight Prayer Battle Gateways," where we stand on guard, alert, watching out for danger, ready and able to defend the gates of our families, homes, streets, neighborhoods, cities, counties, states, and nation from the onslaught and manifestations of demonic entities. Watches, watchers, or watchmen are essentially armed guards. But fear Not!

According to Psalm 149:9, we have been given the honor of executing written judgments against demonic kings and nobles! Do you realize the victory that is already yours to command, control and transform your life? Indeed, you are an overcomer and more than a conqueror, in the mighty name of Jesus!

In the Bible, we learn three main valuable lessons from the ministry of Jesus with regard to His command for us to watch and pray, encapsulated in the following three "A"s:

1. **Awake:** Jesus sometimes prayed all night or woke up early to pray. (Luke 6:12; Mk. 1:35)
2. **Alert:** He received divined verdicts, judgments and empowerments for miracles, signs and wonders from His Father, the Righteous and Just Judge of the entire universe. (John 8:16)
3. **Attack:** By day, He made war by executing the written judgments against the kingdom of darkness. (Casting demons, setting captives free, etc.)

Jesus commands us to be on guard, watch and pray not only because of the activities of Satan and his kingdom of darkness, but also, we as the church, as the ecclesia, have been given powers as restrainers of evil with authority to:

1. Take care of the flock for the Good Shepherd.
2. Take care of ourselves, the body of Christ.
3. Execute the written judgment against the kingdom of darkness.

29

4. Take the good news of the gospel of the Kingdom of God and His Christ to a lost, blind, impoverished and dying world.

5. Set the captives free, break yokes, lift burdens off the weary and harvest souls for the Kingdom of God.

6. To be fruitful, multiply, subdue, and take dominion of this world, delegated to us by God as recorded in the book of Genesis 1:28.

7. Take care of Christ's Kingdom until His return.

Seeking the will of heaven manifested through prayer watches comes with tremendous blessings. Besides, when you watch, not only are you waiting for the Master who has left you in charge of His inheritance, but you also watch that thieves do not steal what has been entrusted to your care, or your watch in this generation for His glory! Remember, God has invested so much including His Kingdom in you therefore watch and pray, and faint not!

The prayers contained in this book are meant to guide you and can be incorporated or modified to suit your current availability and ability to pray.

For the end of the year and beginning of the year prayer watches, you may also get my book, "Battle Of The Kingdoms: End-of-Year & Beginning-of-Year Annual Forty-Day Fasting & Prayer," with over 1600 powerful and anointed prayer points.

CHAPTER 1

FIRST WATCH (6:00 PM – 9:00 PM) TIME FOR DIVINE BEGINNINGS

The Manifestation Of The Fatherhood Of God

The Early Night Watch or The First Watch Of The Night is the hours between 6 PM - 9 PM, signifies the beginning of creation. In our beginning, God created us as a family, in His own image and likeness. He is our heavenly Father and we are His children.

The First Watch connects our destinies to the manifestation of the Fatherhood of God, and the beginning of our earthly time. It is also a time of reflection with Abba Father "and he shall turn the heart of the fathers to the children, and the heart of the children to their fathers," in line with Malachi 4:6.

The First Watch is when you pray for restoration and reconciliation with Abba Father, and our heavenly family. Ask Abba Father to continue to reveal Himself in a more profound and intimate relationship to you. Tap into the fatherhood anointing of Abba Father so that you can be a good father to your own children!

Period For Covenant Renewal With God

It was the watch, during which Jesus broke bread with His covenant between God and Israel. We need to be mindful of the New Covenant and its contents for our lives! Check out the following: Jer. 31:31-34; Matt. 26:28; Heb. 9:15.

It is the time to appropriate, the provisions in the Blood Covenant. Invoke, activate the blessings of the New Everlasting Covenant with its unmerited grace, in which God pledges forgiveness of sins, and His laws written on the hearts and minds of those with trusting faith and repentance, to know Him more closely!

- Every covenant you have with God can be renewed at this time.

Time For The Nature Of The Lamb Of God

This term refers to the ability to do what others can't do (Rev. 5): Behold the Lamb, the Lion of the Tribe of Judah who is able to break every yoke, and seals, and open the Title Deed of the Universe of power, wealth, strength, wisdom, honor, glory and blessings to unlock your destiny!

Leadership is Service: The greatest people lead by example. Humility is the greatest secret of His strength: Jesus tied a towel around His waist and washed the feet of His disciples.

Time For Preservation Of The Fruits Of Your Life.

Every executive/leader can begin to pray for every project he or she starts to live out its divinely ordained lifespan. This **includes** the fruits of the body as well.

Ask the Lord to remove all hindrances against

- Pray for the throne of God to be established in your heart.
- Focus more on praying scripture into the gates.
- Pray for the Lord to take you to His Mountain of Prayer.

Start with thanksgiving, praising and worshipping God. As you worship, read aloud and proclaim Psalm 148, commanding everything in creation to praise God in your life, work/business, family, church and your community and nation.

Pray for repentance on behalf of your family, ministry, workplace, nation, etc. based on such scriptures like Psalms 51, Daniel 9:3-19 and 1 John 1:5 -10.

- Pray and ask Jesus to deal with all wrong foundations in your life.
- Ask for the restoration of heights from which you've fallen.

Declaring, "Father, I repent for my unfaithfulness and disobedience in my covenant with You according to Isaiah. 56:6."

- Invite the Holy Spirit to take absolute control, and lead your prayers.
- Pray for the Kingdom of heaven to permeate your life, and that of your loved ones, your neighborhood, and all other areas, in the mighty name of Jesus.

Cover yourself and your family, ministry, work, property, your neighborhood, city, and nation with the blood of Jesus.

Thy Kingdom Come, Thy Will be done on earth as it is in heaven: What is the difference between the kingdom of God and the Kingdom of heaven, although at times they are interchanged in their usage in the Bible?

The kingdom of God refers to God's authority and rulership, involving the King, His Throne, the Foundations of the Throne (including altars, gates and covenants), the Scepter, the Council of Elders, the Messengers (Men & Angel), and the Subjects or the Ruled; whereas the kingdom of heaven refers to the atmosphere, or culture and place of God's Kingdom.

- Pray and ask the Kingdom of God and of heaven to invade earth on your behalf for the new day.
- Ask that the Kingdom of God to be established in your heart, in the mighty name of Jesus.

It is also the time to pray and silence all the voices (Curses) of the enemy on our life, family, church, city and nation on our new day to harm us.

We must possess the gates of our new day. Otherwise, it will be our enemies possessing them, releasing curses on our day/s. During the beginning of this watch, some witches like dogs go around the precincts of the city (Psalms 59), because they intend to take hold of the gates of the day. It is our responsibility to release judgment on the wicked in alignment of the evening tide as revealed in Isaiah 17:12-14.

Commanding Your Evening

In order to change the spiritual equation, and transform our lives, family, church, city and nation, we need to release and proclaim into the new day God's blessings and grace into our environment before the demons and evil spirits, entities and personalities take control for the Kingdom of Darkness.

Why grace? Jesus did what He was able to do on earth because of the grace of God. Most people have been taught to share the grace at the end of prayers, but actually it's better to ask for and receive the power of God's grace before you embark on anything you do.

Similarly, the importance of taking control and possessing your day and your life starts by commanding your evening. You may have heard of the importance to command your morning but, before commanding your morning make sure you know how to first command your evening, the spiritual gate to your brand-new day!

FIRST WATCH PRAYER POINTS
START PRAYING FROM 5:30 PM

Confession: Psalm 148 (Appendix C)

Psalm 103:1-5 NKJV
"Bless the Lord, O my soul;
And all that is within me, bless His holy name!
Bless the Lord, O my soul,
And forget not all His benefits:
Who forgives all your iniquities,
Who heals all your diseases,
Who redeems your life from destruction,
Who crowns you with lovingkindness and tender mercies,
Who satisfies your mouth with good things,
So that your youth is renewed like the eagle's."

Psalm 5:1-2
"Give ear to my words, O Lord, consider my meditation. Hearken unto the voice of my cry, my King, and my God: for unto thee will I pray."

Psalm 24:7-10
"Lift up your heads, O you gates! And be lifted up, you everlasting doors! And the King of glory shall come in. Who is this King of glory? The Lord strong and mighty, The Lord mighty in battle. Lift up your heads, O you

gates! Lift up, you everlasting doors! And the King of glory shall come in. Who is this King of glory? The Lord of hosts, He is the King of glory."

Lamentations 2:19-20 NKJV
"Arise, cry out in the night, At the beginning of the watches; Pour out your heart like water before the face of the Lord. Lift your hands toward Him For the life of your young children, Who faint from hunger at the head of every street."

"See, O Lord, and consider! To whom have You done this? Should the women eat their offspring, the children they have cuddled? Should the priest and prophet be slain in the sanctuary of the Lord?"

Isaiah. 17:12-14
"Woe to the multitude of many people Who make a noise like the roar of the seas, And to the rushing of nations That make a rushing like the rushing of mighty waters! The nations will rush like the rushing of many waters; But God will rebuke them, and they will flee far away, And be chased like the chaff of the mountains before the wind. Like a rolling thing before the whirlwind. Then behold, at eventide, trouble! And before the morning, he is no more. This is the portion of those who plunder us, And the lot of those who rob us."

Personal Prayer Of:
- Thanksgiving, Praise and Worship,
- Repentance and Forgiveness of Sin, Transgression, and Iniquities of your bloodline
- Empowerment by the Holy Spirit;

- Pleading, Activation and the validation of the power of the Blood of Jesus, and of the Lamb.

I Decree and declare the times of refreshing into my life, family, and into all areas and pillars of society including:

- Government and policy making
- Media and entertainment including print, electronic,
- Drama and theatre, holiday and leisure activities.
- Family
- The priesthood of God
- Stewardship and finances
- Welfare and justice
- Education
- The belief system and mindset of the people toward God and His Word.

1. Abba Father, let the manifestation of Your Fatherhood deal with all wrong foundations in my life. I ask for the restoration of heights from which I have fallen from Your image and likeness, in the mighty name of Jesus.
2. Father, deal with all wrong foundations in my life, my family, in the church, government, economy, science and technology, formal schools, the media, arts, sports and culture, in the mighty name of Jesus.
3. I TAKE <u>DOMINION</u> and nullify all the curses that the enemy has released on this new day: on my life, my family, church, city, state, and this nation, in the mighty name of Jesus Christ of Nazareth.

4. God, may all those who oppose us and are planning evil activities to harm us at the midnight hour, fall to nothing, as I pray and cripple all the effects of the satanic prophets and priests in the land, in the mighty name of Jesus.

5. I pray for the night to come over their eyes so their vision and declarations will be futile, in the mighty name of Jesus.

6. I pray for the judgment of the Lord upon the spirits of wickedness in the land, pertaining to strongholds of false religions, divinations, idols, shrines, necromancy, water spirits, witchcraft, according to Isaiah 17:12-14 and Isaiah 42:18-22, in the mighty name of Jesus.

7. Lord of Hosts come and take hold of the gates of this nation and by the working of Your mighty strength paralyze all the strongholds of the devil, so that Jesus alone will be enthroned in this family, church, school, neighborhood, city, state, and nation, in the mighty name of Jesus. (Psalm. 45:4)

8. Let all my spiritual, ancient gates and everlasting doors, bow to King Jesus, The Lord of Hosts, strong and mighty in battle, in the mighty name of Jesus!

9. I command them to open so that the King of Glory with His blood and glory and His light can come in and possess and reign my new day, in Jesus' mighty name.

10. Father, send Your angels to operate these gates so they can release godliness and righteousness into my life, family, city and nation, in Jesus' mighty name.

11. Father, open all these ancient gates in this nation so that only the forces of God, Light and Heaven, with the keys of David can enter so no foreign elements, spiritual or physical can gain access to harm, or sway anyone, in the mighty name of Jesus.

12. Father, by the spirit of the Eveningtide, I close the night, and the past upon the activities of my enemies, and usher a new refreshing season in my life, family, church, nation, in the mighty name of Jesus.

13. Father, I repent for my unfaithfulness and disobedience in my covenant with You according to Your Word in Isaiah. 56:6, in the mighty name of Jesus.

14. Abba Father, by the power of the Holy Spirit, I ask for and receive grace to hold fast to my covenant with You, in the mighty name of Jesus.

15. I pray that all satanic covenants and altars in our families and in the church of Jesus Christ will be wiped out, so that God's original covenants can be renewed, in the mighty name of Jesus. (Zech. 13:1-2).

16. Father, may Your original covenant blessings with us, be activated and experienced by Your people, in the mighty name of Jesus.

17. Lamb of God, break every yoke of bondage in my life and the nation, and grant me the <u>Title Deed of the Universe</u> of power, wealth, strength, wisdom, honor, glory and blessings, according to Rev. 5:10-12. Amen!

18. I decree and ordain for every project I have started to live out its divinely ordained lifespan, in Jesus' mighty name.

19. God, enlighten our spiritual eyes and give us access to the spiritual gates as established by the enemy in the land, in the mighty name of Jesus.

20. May the judgment of God strike all the thrones of iniquity in our nation, cultural, and racial groups in our societies, etc., and issues that proceed from these thrones be cut off, in the mighty name of Jesus.

21. Father, may Your Presence transform the spiritual, socioeconomic, political, and cultural landscape in this nation, in this season, in the mighty name of Jesus.

22. I speak healing and reconciliation of all things in the beginning of the new season in my life, my family, my nation back to You Abba Father, according to Colossians 1:15-19, in the mighty name of Jesus.

23. I decree that no backlash of the enemy will come upon my life, family, nation and the body of Christ, in the mighty name of Jesus.

24. Abba Father, I praise and extol You in this new season of time- for Thine is the Kingdom, the Power and the Glory, forever and ever, in the mighty name of Jesus. Amen.

"Be persistent and devoted to prayer, being alert and focused in your prayer life with an attitude of thanksgiving."

(Colossians 4:2 AMP)

CHAPTER 2

SECOND WATCH (9:00 PM - 12 MIDNIGHT) DIVINE VISITATION AND FAVOR

Pray For Divine Favor

SECOND WATCH OF THE NIGHT is period between 9:00Pm and 12 Midnight. If you read Exodus 3:21- 22; 11:3-4; 12:35-36; you will see that God made the Egyptians favorably disposed towards the Israelites so that the Egyptians gave whatever they asked from them. This favor was after supper, after the Passover feast, between 9.00 pm and 12.00 midnight before the angel of death passed through Egypt and no one could go on to the neighbors.

It was at the midnight hour that God struck down the first-born of Egypt, which resulted in His people being released from captivity and set free to worship Him. In ancient Egyptian society, the first-born male was the pride of their inheritance in their culture.

- Ask God to humble every pride of ancient Egyptian and their Pharaoh, and their taskmasters bent on keeping you and your family in captivity, in all areas and realms of your lives.

This is the time for:

- respect from men.
- plundering your oppressors.
- favor from men.

In Acts 23:23, we see Paul enjoying favor from the captain of the soldiers during this period. The same army general who had arrested Paul, now ended up protecting Paul! As you pray today,

- God will cause you to have favor in the eyes of your enemies.
- God would cause the people who have arrested us before, to protect His purpose for our lives.

It has been said that what the governor could not enjoy was given to Paul. He was given 470 soldiers as an escort!

"This watch is a time when God judges the enemies who are trying to keep us from entering into His perfect plan for our lives."

Psalm 119:62 says,

"At midnight I will rise to give thanks to You because of Your righteous judgments."

The Outpouring Of The Spirit Of Prayer
Pray For The Outpouring Of The Spirit Of Prayer Upon You And The

Church And Your Nation. Disaster was imminent, and yet the disciples, could not watch and pray! With the spirit of prayer during **this watch, intercessors are able to impact the** spiritual realm before the enemy gets ready to wreak havoc.

Recall that on the day Jesus was betrayed, He started praying for God's grace at 9.00 pm. It is the time to pray for the release or outpouring of the Spirit of Grace, of Prayer and Supplication. (Matt. 26:33)

- At 10.00 pm, He came back to His disciples and said, "Could you not watch with me one hour?"
- At 11.00 pm, He came a second time and said "Are you still sleeping?" He left them and went back.
- Then the third time that was 12 midnight, He said, "Rise, and let us go for my betrayer is at hand."
- This period is the time to pray for strength against all temptation and trials.
- Pray for double stamina to watch and persevere in prayer! (Zechariah. 9:12)

Pray For Divine Protection

(Psalm 3:1-7; 17:8-14, Acts 23:23; Zechariah 1:10)

Your mind is a battlefield! Therefore:

- Be alert as to what you see.
- Be sensitive to what you read, or what movies and Television shows you watch.
- Be careful of what music you listen to, and the people who have your ear.

Prime time for Television shows: It has been said that Hollywood prefers to show all the evil films to make provision for your being affected in the next watch!

- Watch out! What shows do you love to watch? Be alert, be on guard!
- Don't be addicted to movies with demonic themes such as witchcraft, sorcery or shows laced with erotic and immoral decadence.
- Above all, don't let pride in your heart! Guard your heart!
- Be careful and be spiritually sensitive because people tend to worship whoever or whatever they adore!

Therefore, open the gate of your heart and adore Jesus and focus on the Kingdom of God, and of Heaven! Watch the gates to your soul and shut them tight against the enemy, or else he would steal, kill, and destroy your destiny! (John 10:10)

Angelic Visitation Escort And Protection

"This is also the period to pray and ask for the release of the troops of God to be on patrol and give angelic escort."

(Acts 9:23).

"And the man who stood among the myrtle trees answered and said, These are the ones whom the Lord has sent to walk to and fro throughout the earth."

(Zechariah 1:10 NKJV)

- Night vigils attract angelic presence and assistance.
- An Angel was sent to release Peter from prison.

- Pray and invoke the partnership and assistance of angelic escort and protection.

Fear Not! God's eyes are upon you and He is saying,

"Then I will encamp about My house as a guard or a garrison so that none shall march back and forth, and no oppressor or demanding collector shall again overrun them, for now My eyes are upon them."

(Zechariah 9:8AMP)

Prayer For Provision To Do God's Work

Pray for spiritual and physical provisions (strength, abilities, freedom from all limitations). (Exo.3:21-22, 11:3-4, 12:35-36, Psalm 5:12; 45:12; Esther 2:9- 17).

- Time to ask for the supply of all resources, tools, and weapons needed for every God-given project. (see Exo 12:35, 36).

It was at this time that the Israelites got everything from the Egyptians that they needed to build the Tabernacle in the wilderness. Pray for the release of provisions at this time.

This is also the watch to pray for the sense of urgency to accomplish whatever God wants you to do. For example:

- The Israelites ate the Passover standing with their tunics tucked with belts ready to move!

Warfare Prayer For The Nation

Intercede for your neighborhood, city, state, and nation!

During the night hours, fewer prayers go to the Throne room. Therefore, pray that God will overthrow all satanic activities released to attack our communities, cities and the nation, so that God's peace and purposes will be experienced in our lives as written,

"Therefore He knows their works; He overthrows them in the night, And they are crushed." (Job 34:25NKJV)

Why Pray For Your Environment?

Why pray for your environment and even that of your enemies? For your own peace and safety! God commands us to pray for the welfare of our dwelling places, city, state and nation saying,

"And seek the peace of the city where I have caused you to be carried away captive, and pray to the Lord for it; for in its peace you will have peace."

(Jeremiah 29:7NKJV)

SECOND WATCH PRAYER POINTS
START PRAYING FROM 8:30 PM

Confession: Psalm 148, Psalm 59, (see Bible Verses)

Psalm 68:1-4

"Let God arise, Let His enemies be scattered; Let those also who hate Him flee before Him. As smoke is driven away, So drive them away; As wax melts before the fire, So let the wicked perish at the presence of God. But let the righteous be glad; Let them rejoice before God; Yes, let them rejoice exceedingly. Sing to God, sing praises to His name; extol Him, by His name YAH; rejoice before Him."

Isaiah 8:9-10

"Associate yourselves, O ye people, and ye shall be broken in pieces; and give ear, all ye of far countries: gird yourselves, and ye shall be broken in pieces; gird yourselves, and ye shall be broken in pieces. Take counsel together, and it shall come to nought; speak the word, and it shall not stand: for God is with us."

Personal Prayer Of

- Thanksgiving, Praise and Worship,
- Repentance and Forgiveness of Sin,
- Empowerment by the Holy Spirit;
- Pleading and Activation of the power of the Blood of Jesus.

1. Let the favor of the Lord be upon me and my family, in the mighty name of Jesus. (Psalm. 15:12).

2. Let God plunder all my oppressors so that my household lacks no good thing, in the mighty name of Jesus.

3. I will not miss the hour of my favor and visitation, in the mighty name of Jesus. (Exodus. 3:22)

4. Let every limitation of my gifts and abilities in God be lifted, in the mighty name of Jesus.

5. Father, make my enemies favorably disposed towards me so that their own testimony of me will extend tremendous goodwill towards me today, in Jesus' mighty name.

6. Abba Father, release Your favor, protection and preservation into the foundations of my families, communities and the church as a whole, in the mighty name of Jesus (Acts 23:23-31; Esther 2:9).

7. Holy Spirit, pour the spirit and stamina of prayer upon me and the Church in this city, in Jesus' mighty name.

8. Father, continue to pour upon us the Spirit of Grace and Supplication to overcome temptations and trials, in the mighty name of Jesus.

9. Father, release a host of angels to usher my family and I into our place of rest in Your providence, in the mighty name of Jesus.

10. Let the arrows of weariness, frustration and failure, fired against me at the altar of prayer backfire and destroy their senders! In the mighty name of Jesus.

11. Lord, keep me safe from all harm; from the arrow that flies by day and the pestilence at night, in the mighty name of Jesus.

12. Lord, smash every syndicate of conspirators and quicken my deliverance from the forces of hell, and hades, in the mighty name of Jesus

13. God, deal with Your enemies, so that Your people can possess, their inheritance, in Jesus' mighty name.

14. Almighty God, our source of all divine provisions, pour upon Your Church abundant resources for all Kingdom projects, in the mighty name of Jesus. (Exo. 11:3-4)

15. Holy Spirit, empower the church into battle against the forces of hell, so that the battle will be taken to the enemy's gates, in the mighty name of Jesus. (Matthew. 16:18-20).

16. God, cause the enemies of the church of Jesus Christ to begin to promote God's prophetic purposes for the Church, in the mighty name of Jesus (Exodus 11:3-4; 3:20-21).

17. Father, arise and overthrow all satanic activities released to attack our communities, cities and the nation, so that peace and Your purposes will be experienced, in the mighty name of Jesus.

18. Abba Father, send forth Your mighty angels to arrest wicked spirits sent out to devastate the land and the people, in the mighty name of Jesus.

19. God, come to this city in Your glory, so that all the powers, principalities and wicked spirits that torment the people will be chased out of town, in the mighty name Jesus. (Exodus. 11:4)

20. May the judgment of God strike all the thrones of iniquity in our nation, regions and society; and may all the issues that proceed from these thrones be cut off, in the mighty name of Jesus.

21. Father, I declare restoration, the glory and the blessings of the Lord upon the 8 pillars of society, and the people of the land, in the mighty name of Jesus.

22. I speak healing and reconciliation of all things in the beginning of the new season in my life, my family, my nation, back to You Abba Father, according to Colossians 1:15-19, in the mighty name of Jesus.

23. I decree that no backlash of the enemy will come upon my life, family, nation and the body of Christ, in the mighty name of Jesus.

24. Abba Father, I praise and extol You in this new season of time- for Thine is the Kingdom, the Power and the Glory, forever and ever, in the mighty name of Jesus. Amen.

CHAPTER 3

THIRD WATCH (12:00 AM – 3:00 AM) JUSTICE WARFARE AND DELIVERANCE

Time For Spiritual Warfare.

THE MIDNIGHT WATCH OR THIRD WATCH OF THE NIGHT is the hours between 12 midnight to 3:00 am. In spiritual warfare, midnight is of strategic importance. Why? Midnight is a period of heightened satanic activities. The key is to first direct your prayers toward the ancestral roots of your birth, and second, the current place of your domicile. Therefore, if you were born in Europe, Africa, or Asia, but lives in the United States of America, you have two midnights to do battle!

Keeping prayer vigils between midnight and dawn is best because it disrupts the meetings and activities of the enemy. It is at these meetings that our enemies meet to deliver their reports, re-strategies and take decisions concerning the destiny of many, including Christians.

It is also the time they analyze the effectiveness of burdens, and punishment already placed on their victims, or assigns, enforce and supervise new yokes and afflictions.

You have the power to determine their fate before they determine yours. How? Through night vigils, and by going on your knees and scattering their meetings, tearing down their strongholds in the heavenlies, and stripping them powerless, before they have the opportunity to fulfill their assignments to fight against you during the day.

Ask Samson, and he will tell you what he did at midnight as written:

"And Samson lay low till midnight; then he arose at midnight, took hold of the doors of the gate of the city and the two gateposts, pulled them up, bar and all, put them on his shoulders, and carried them to the top of the hill that faces Hebron."

(Judges 16:3)

Why is the Third Watch of the night one of the most important times to keep watch? Here is why!

- Remember, in Matthew 13:25, while men slept the enemy went to sow tares.
- This is when the deep sleep falls upon men, according to Acts 20:7-12.
- The devil operates at this time when men are sleeping, and there are not many people praying to oppose him. (Matt. 13:24; 1 King 3:20)
- The third watch is the major time when witches offer sacrifices and invoke covenants.

Pray and issue decrees of judgment against their evil altars as written:

"And, behold, there came a man of God out of Judah by the word of the Lord unto Bethel: and Jeroboam stood by the altar to burn incense. And he cried against the altar in the word of the Lord, and said, O altar, altar, thus saith the Lord; Behold, a child shall be born unto the house of David, Josiah by name; and upon thee shall he offer the priests of the high places that burn incense upon thee, and men's bones shall be burnt upon thee."

(1 Kings 13:1-2)

Give ear, O ye heavens, and I will speak, hear, O earth, the utterances of the word of the Most High God, the God of Abraham, the God of Isaac, the God of Jacob and Israel, the Righteous and Just Judge of the Universe, in my mouth; O altar, altar, you evil witchcraft altar of my bloodline, thus saith the Lord, upon thee shall I slaughter the priests of the high places that burn incense and make sacrifices upon thee, in the mighty name of Jesus.

Time For Slaying

It is also the time when the destroying angel goes through the enemy's camp, neighborhood, community, city, or nation (Exodus 12:29, 2Kings 19:35).

- The nighttime is a time for angelic intervention. In one night, an angel wiped out 185,000 men of Sennacherib's army.
- This is also the time the wicked are wiped out. (Isaiah 17:14; Exodus 12:29)

The unseen evil wicked enemies also plan accidents, loss of jobs, thefts, deaths, and other calamities, to ruin your day.

Time to declare Psalm 91:5, 6 for divine protection for yourself, family, church, neighborhood, city and nation.

It is this period that rapists increase their activity, according to Judges 19:25. The Levite's concubine was raped about this period and was only left to go before dawn, so pray and silence all spiritual rapists.

"But the men would not heed him. So the man took his concubine, and brought her out to them. And they knew her and abused her all night until morning; and when the day began to break, they let her go."

(Judges 19:25NKJV)

But don't be anxious for as written:

"Though the cords of the wicked have enclosed and ensnared me, I have not forgotten Your law. At midnight I will rise to give thanks to You because of Your righteous ordinances."

(Psalm 119:61-62)

Night Vigil Prayers

Midnight is also symbolic of intense darkness, but God is Light and darkness cannot overcome light.

Pray for knowledge, ask God to release strategies to you during this time,

"For it is ... God who commanded light to shine out of darkness, who has shone in our hearts to give the light of the knowledge of the glory of God in the face of Jesus Christ."

(2 Corinthians 4:6)

- Command the glory light of Jesus to shine through your darkest hour of need or desperation.
- Command light to shine out of your darkness!
- Command light to reveal and destroy the enemy's activities.

Time Of Release From Every Prison

(Isa. 42:22; Jud. 16:3; Acts 16:25; Ps. 18:27-28)

- Pray for angelic presence and intervention.
- This is also the time people are generally released.

"God released the people of Israel to leave Egypt at this time. Remember, it was also at midnight that Samson carried the gates of the city and went out."

(Judges 16:3)

- You can possess the gates of your enemies with your mouth and prayers!

Paul and Silas were released as written,

"But at midnight Paul and Silas were praying and singing hymns to God, and the prisoners were listening to them. Suddenly there was a great earthquake, so that the foundations of the prison were shaken; and immediately all the doors were opened and everyone's chains were loosed." (Acts 16:25-26NKJV)

- This is a special time for divine government to overrule human decrees! (Exodus. 12 - 14).
- Implore the Lord to judge for you. (Psalm 119:62)

- The Lord will empower you to rule in the midst of your enemies. (Psalm 110)

Freedom From Spiritual Marriage

- This is the watch to pray for freedom from spiritual marriages or illicit sexual encounters, in your life; especially, in your dreams and nightmares.

Romancing And Having Sex In Your Dreams?

The account of the gang-rape of the concubine in the book of Judges happened physically, but it also happens spiritually. Be warned, all sexual encounters in your dream should be a source of concern to you. Pray and cancel any evil deposits or attack to manipulate you!

Seeking marriage partners: According to Matthew. 25:6, it was at midnight that the Bridegroom came. In the case of Ruth, though she had been sleeping at Boaz's feet, it was at midnight that he noticed that a woman was sleeping there. (Ruth 3:8)

- Pray that God will cause your family, the Church, city, and other institutions, or endeavors, etc. to be noticed at this time.
- Those of you who are not married, or who are trusting God for marriage partners, this is a good time to pray to also get married.
- For those who are married, this is probably the best time to pray for your marriage.
- Pray for the discovery of new and beautiful things in your spouse.
- Pray for Abba Father to show you things to make your marriage a happy one (Ruth 3:1-10).

A Robber vs. A Thief

We are warned to be awake, alert, watch out, and be ready to defend our possessions through prayer. According to Jesus,

"The thief cometh not, but for to steal, and to kill, and to destroy: I am come that they might have life, and that they might have it more abundantly."

(John 10:10)

He also said,

"Verily, verily, I say unto you, He that entereth not by the door into the sheepfold, but climbeth up some other way, the same is a thief and a robber."

(John 10:1)

What is the difference between a robber and a thief?

- The difference between robbers and thieves is that robbers rob in daylight; thieves steal when you are unaware!

The thief and the robber are equal opportunity employees of the kingdom of darkness and have been robbing and stealing from us since the fall of mankind in the Garden of Eden. Beware of thieves at all times, but more so at night! This period is also the watch to keep the prayer lamps burning to brighten your spiritual realm and expose the activities of the kingdom of darkness warring against you. Thank God and say,

"For You will light my lamp; Lord my God will enlighten my darkness."

(Psa. 18: 28)

- Watch, for the thief comes when it is dark, and when you are tired, asleep, unprepared, and unsecured. (Matthew 24:43)
- Watch! Awake!! Alert And Attack!!!

The Best Times To Make Your Case In Prayer

- Pray and make your case in prayer. "**At midnight** I will rise to give thanks unto thee because of **thy righteous judgments**." (Psalm 119:62)
- This is also the period to pray for God to release every emergency provision in your life.
- Don't give up so easily. Press on, persist and persevere to the end!

God loves us and so He commands us to persevere, even as we present our prayers and petitions to Him. He says,

"I have set watchmen on your walls, O Jerusalem; They shall never hold their peace day or night. You who make mention of the Lord, do not keep silent, And give Him no rest till He establishes and till He makes Jerusalem a praise in the earth."

(Isaiah 62:6-7NKJV)

Jesus also commands us to pray and not lose heart even in our midnight hours until our prayers are answered saying:

"Which of you shall have a friend, and go to him at midnight and say to him, 'Friend, lend me three loaves;' I say to you, though he will not rise and give to him because he is his friend, yet because of his persistence he will rise and give him as many as he needs."

(Lk. 11:5-13)

Midnight Is Also:

- Time for miracles or covenants (Acts 20:7-12)

- Time to apply the Blood of Jesus to wipe out and render powerless every ordinance written in the heavens, in the waters, in the high places and by the astrologers and witches, in this new season.

- A time to awake out of sleep and confront every storm of destruction and distraction in your life, your family and your ministry. (Acts 16:25-34)

- It is the time to speak peace and calm into every situation of turbulence and confusion.

- When most dreams occur (Job 33:15-16). Dreams and visions alert us to spiritual activities.

THIRD WATCH PRAYER POINTS
START PRAYING FROM 11:30 PM

Confession: Ps 148, Isaiah 44:24-28, Isaiah 19:1-4, Isaiah 8:9-10

Isaiah 44:24-28 NKJV

"Thus says the Lord, your Redeemer, And He who formed you from the womb: "I am the Lord, who makes all things, Who stretches out the heavens all alone, Who spreads abroad the earth by Myself; Who frustrates the signs of the babblers, And drives diviners mad; Who turns wise men backward, And makes their knowledge foolishness; Who confirms the word of His servant, And performs the counsel of His messengers; Who says to Jerusalem, 'You shall be inhabited,' To the cities of Judah, 'You shall be built,' And I will raise up her waste places; Who says to the deep, 'Be dry! And I will dry up your rivers'; who says of Cyrus, 'He is My shepherd, And he shall perform all My pleasure, Saying to Jerusalem, "You shall be built," And to the temple, "Your foundation shall be laid.""""

Isaiah 19:1-4 NKJV

"The burden against Egypt: Behold, the Lord rides on a swift cloud, And will come into Egypt; The idols of Egypt will totter at His presence, And the heart of Egypt will melt in its midst. "I will set Egyptians against Egyptians; Everyone will fight against his brother, And everyone against his neighbor, City against city, kingdom against kingdom. The spirit of Egypt will fail in its midst; I will destroy their counsel, And they will consult the idols and the charmers, The mediums and the sorcerers. And the Egyptians I will give Into the hand of a cruel master, And a fierce king will rule over them," Says the Lord, the Lord of hosts."

Isaiah 8:9-10 NKJV

"Be shattered, O you peoples, and be broken in pieces! Give ear, all you from far countries. Gird yourselves, but be broken in pieces; Gird yourselves, but be broken in pieces. Take counsel together, but it will come to nothing; Speak the word, but it will not stand, For God is with us."

Personal Prayer Of

- Thanksgiving, Praise and Worship,
- Repentance and Forgiveness of Sin,
- Empowerment by the Holy Spirit;
- Pleading and Activation of the power of the Blood of Jesus.

1. Abba Father, overthrow all satanic activities released to attack our communities, cities and the nation, so that peace and Your purposes alone will be experienced in our cities and nation, in the mighty name of Jesus (Job 34:25; Jer. 29:7).
2. Father, send forth Your mighty angels to arrest wicked spirits sent out to devastate the land and the people, in the mighty name of Jesus.
3. Abba, Father, come in Your glory, so all the powers; principalities and wicked spirits that torment the people will be chased out of town, in the mighty name of Jesus (Exodus. 11:4).
4. Lord, I plead the Kingdom of Heaven to unravel insights and revelations to me, in the mighty name of Jesus.

5. May the Lord ride forth victoriously on behalf of truth; humility and righteousness against those who fight and oppress my life, family, job, finances, ministry, and the Church, in the mighty name of Jesus. (Psalm 45:4)

6. Father, arrest every thief sent out to steal from my barn today, in the mighty name of Jesus.

7. Thus says the Lord, "Let My people go!" Therefore, every Pharaoh holding me, and my family in bondage, may your firstborn son die, in the mighty name of Jesus. (Exodus. 4:22-23).

8. I break loose and throw away all the shackles of anti-progress and prosperity in my life and family, in the mighty name of Jesus.

9. Father, I pray that You will lead the Church to subdue all spiritual and physical strongholds that constitute the kingdom of darkness affecting my life and this nation, in the mighty name of Jesus. (Psalm 60:9, 10).

10. Lord, may the Church and its leadership be released from all satanic manipulations, in the mighty name of Jesus (Acts 16:25; Judges 16:3).

11. Father, deliver us from spiritual drowsiness, and raise us as prayer warriors empowered to watch and pray without ceasing, in the mighty name of Jesus. (Acts 20:7-12)

12. Father, empower me to resist, and break off every evil spiritual marriage, suitors, and spouses, in the mighty name of Jesus.

13. Abba Father, bless us Your children, with blessings of heaven above, and the blessings of the deep that lies beneath, in the mighty name of Jesus. (Gen. 49:25-26)

14. I decree and declare the divine protection of Psalms 91: 5-6 that states "You shall not be afraid of the terror by night, Nor of the arrow that flies by day, Nor of the pestilence that walks in

darkness, Nor of the destruction that lays waste at noonday," upon my life and that of my family, in the mighty name of Jesus.

15. I apply the Blood of Jesus and wipe out every ordinance written in the heavens, in the waters, in the high places against my destiny, and my family, in the mighty name of Jesus.

16. Dream attackers and manipulators, I soak my dreams in the blood of Jesus, die, in the mighty name of Jesus.

17. I shall have sweet dreams, and the flow of beautiful messages of revelation during this hour from God, in the mighty name of Jesus.

18. FATHER, many Christians have been plundered, looted and locked up in spiritual and physical prison houses. Father, send Your scouting and warring angels to release and set them free in the Lord, in the mighty name of Jesus (Isa. 42:18-22, Matt. 27:15).

19. May the angel of the Lord destroy the camp of the wicked as in the days of Sennacherib's defeat and death, in the mighty name of Jesus. (2 Kings 19:35)

20. Abba Father, bless my marriage abundantly, and grant the request of those looking for spousal mates according to Ruth 3: 1-10; Matthew 25:6, in Jesus' mighty name.

21. I command any blood sacrificed against my family, and my destiny be reversed by fire, in Jesus' mighty name.

22. I speak healing and reconciliation of all things in the beginning of the new season in my life, my family, and our nation back to You, Father, according to Colossians 1:15-19, in the mighty name of Jesus.

23. I decree that no backlash of the enemy will come upon my life, family, nation and the body of Christ, in the mighty name of Jesus.

24. Abba Father, I praise and extol You in this new season of time- for Thine is the Kingdom, the Power and the Glory, forever and ever, in the mighty name of Jesus. Amen.

CHAPTER 4

FOURTH WATCH (3:00 AM-6:00 AM) RELEASE OF DIVINE JUDGMENTS

A Time To Ambush Your Attackers

THE FOURTH WATCH OR THE DAWN OR EARLY MORNING WATCH is characterized by great transformation.

The Fourth Watch is always important because this is the last watch/lap of the night battle. This was when Israel was finally released from the clutches of Egypt and her idols. (Exodus 14)

- This is the last watch of the night.
- A time to strike a death blow to stubborn pursuers.
- A time to embrace resurrection power.
- A time to command your morning

This watch is the time that those satanic agents who went out to perform their activities are returning back to their bases. It is essential that the devil and his cohorts run back to 'home base' so that they are not caught by the dayspring.

This is also the watch to release judgments on the wicked, who remain stiff-necked after many warnings and rebukes as written:

"He, that being often reproved hardeneth his neck, shall suddenly be destroyed, and that without remedy."

(Prov. 29:1)

Just as Pharaoh's army was destroyed at the Red Sea:

- Command the East Wind of God to smash and clear your life of any evil impediments; and sweep away as chaff those who stubbornly pursue you, in the mighty name of Jesus Christ of Nazareth.

Pray for every enemy's chariot wheels to be removed as recorded in the book of Exodus 14:24-28.

"Then the Lord said to Moses, "Stretch out your hand over the sea, that the waters may come back upon the Egyptians, on their chariots, and on their horsemen."

(Exodus 14:26NKJV)

- Pray that all stubborn spiritual pursuers and their human agents, all their plans, programs and policies should backfire on them.
- Command the enemy to be totally broken before you and never to rise up against you or your family, or your ministry, in the name of Jesus.

Commanding Your Morning

Just as the evening watch is the gateway to the night hours, so is the fourth watch the gateway to your daytime hours.

By commanding your evening and your morning, you take control of your night and your day to release the blessings of God's promises not only in your life, but to also possess the gates of your enemies to silence their voices and shut down their activities against you and your family.

The Mystery And Power Of The Dayspring

What is the Dayspring?

Though some scholars believe the Dayspring falls between 12 midnight, stretching up to 6.00 am, the full impact of its intensity is felt in the final watch of this period (3.00 - 6.00 am) when <u>it begins to shake everything out</u>.

Do you know how to release the manifestation of the full intensity of the Dayspring to shake out the wicked? God questioned Job:

"Hast thou commanded the morning since thy days; and caused the Dayspring to know his place; That it might take hold of the ends of the earth, that the wicked might be shaken out of it?"

(Job 38:12-13).

Testimonies of former witches converted to Christianity attest to this phenomenon. They tell of experiences, where when they went out of their bodies on witchcraft operation, they had to return into their bodies before sunrise, otherwise they wouldn't have been able to do so. This is because they will have been arrested and shaken out by the Dayspring in line with

Job 38:13 as quoted above. This explains why the agents of the kingdom of darkness and those linked with Satan, heighten their activities, especially between the hours of 12 midnight and 3.00 a.m., knowing that by the next watch (3.00 am - 6.00 am) they'll have to cease their activities lest they will be caught by the full intensity of the Dayspring.

It must be because no spirit is supposed to remain in this state by daybreak, we see this demonstrated by Jacob's encounter with the Angel of the Lord in Genesis 32:24-30.

"Then Jacob was left alone; and a Man wrestled with him until the breaking of day. Now when He saw that He did not prevail against him … He said, "Let Me go, for the day breaks." But he said, "I will not let You go unless You bless me!"

(Genesis. 32:24-26)

The significance of the Fourth Watch can be seen in Mark 1:35, where we see Jesus rising up before daybreak, and finding a solitary place to pray and take command of the day before it begins.

- Command the Dayspring to shake out the wicked!
- Put on your royal and priestly garments and begin to legally command your morning and life; with powerful positive decrees and declarations based on the Word before daybreak!

Deliverance From Enslavement

This is time for deliverance according to Exo. 12 and 14.

"And Moses said to the people, "Do not be afraid. Stand still, and see the salvation of the Lord, which He will accomplish for you today. For the

Egyptians whom you see today, you shall see again no more forever. The Lord will fight for you, and you shall hold your peace."

(Exodus 14:13-14)

Command and release peace and calm in every stormy situation in your life, and that of your family. Just as Jesus, the Prince of Peace came walking on the stormy water to the disciples during this watch according to Matthew 14:25, command your peace to be still, in Jesus' name.

God's Covenant With The Day And The Night

God has covenanted with His creation the day and the night for specific purposes. Learn what they are, respect and obey them!

"Thus says the Lord: 'If My covenant is not with day and night, and if I have not appointed the ordinances of heaven and earth."

(Jeremiah 33:25NKJV)

"Thus saith the Lord; If ye can break my covenant of the day, and my covenant of the night, and that there should not be day and night in their season,"

(Jeremiah 33:20)

In Genesis 8:22, God reminds us that "While the earth remaineth, seedtime and harvest, and cold and heat, and summer and winter, and day and night shall not cease."

In Psalm 19:1-2 we read, "The heavens declare the glory of God; And the firmament shows His handiwork. Day unto day utters speech, And night unto night reveals knowledge."

What do you do with revealed truth? Do you know how to command the day to speak favorably and the night to reveal hidden knowledge and secrets into your life; to transform your situation, your destiny, and those around you, your loved ones and for the general good? It's simple!

Decree and declare the Word and command the new day to speak into your life according to God's promises, plan and purpose for your life, in Jesus' name.

By the power of the Holy Spirit, invoke and tap into God's covenant ordinances with the Day and Night to speak and reveal knowledge, wisdom, guidelines, instructions, special assignments and understanding to cause God's Will to manifest and bless you,

"With blessings of heaven above, Blessings of the deep that lies beneath,.." in the mighty name of Jesus.

(Ps. 19:2, NIV; Genesis 49:25NKJV)

Tap Into Resurrection Power

It was during this watch that the stone in front of the tomb of Jesus was rolled away.

- Pray for all reproach in your life to be rolled away.
- Pray that everything that has died in your life, family, neighborhood, city, State, and nation in terms of potentials, be released, in Jesus' name.
- In God and with God there is no death, but life, vitality and power!
- Pray for the resurrection of dormant and redemptive gifts to rise and shine. (Isa. 60:1-5).

Rise And Shine

Immediately after this watch the sun rises, and shines. Jesus is our Resurrection and our Morning Star to brighten our darkness. As written:

"For thou wilt light my candle: The Lord my God will enlighten my darkness."

(Psalm. 18:28)

Ask the Lord to light the candle of your family, church, school, ministry, association, society, community, neighborhood, city, state, nation or country to rise and shine.

All this information has been made available for you to equip and prepare you in anticipation of the Kingdom of heaven to invade earth on your behalf, in alignment to the portion of the prayer Jesus taught His disciples concerning the Father's Will, saying:

"YOUR WILL BE DONE ON EARTH AS IT IS IN HEAVEN..."

FOURTH WATCH PRAYER POINTS
START PRAYING FROM 2:30AM

Confession: Ps. 148 (see Bible Verses)

Psalm 5:1-3
"Give ear to my words, O Lord, consider my meditation. Hearken unto the voice of my cry, my King, and my God: for unto thee will I pray. My voice shalt thou hear in the morning, O Lord; in the morning will I direct my prayer unto thee, and will look up."

Exodus14:24-28, NIV
"During the last watch of the night the LORD looked down from the pillar of fire and cloud at the Egyptian army and threw it into confusion. He jammed the wheels of their chariots so that they had difficulty driving. And the Egyptians said, "Let's get away from the Israelites! The LORD is fighting for them against Egypt."

Then the LORD said to Moses, "Stretch out your hand over the sea so that the waters may flow back over the Egyptians and their chariots and horsemen." …

The water flowed back and covered the chariots and horsemen-the entire army of Pharaoh that had followed the Israelites into the sea. Not one of them survived."

Isaiah 60:1-5 NKJV

"Arise, shine; For your light has come! And the glory of the Lord is risen upon you. For behold, the darkness shall cover the earth, And deep darkness the people; But the Lord will arise over you, And His glory will be seen upon you. The Gentiles shall come to your light, And kings to the brightness of your rising. "Lift up your eyes all around, and see: They all gather together, they come to you; Your sons shall come from afar, And your daughters shall be nursed at your side. Then you shall see and become radiant; your heart shall swell with joy; Because the abundance of the sea shall be turned to you, The wealth of the Gentiles shall come to you."

Isaiah 62:1-12 NKJV

"For Zion's sake I will not hold My peace,
And for Jerusalem's sake I will not rest,
Until her righteousness goes forth as brightness,
And her salvation as a lamp that burns.
The Gentiles shall see your righteousness,
And all kings your glory.
You shall be called by a new name,
Which the mouth of the Lord will name.
You shall also be a crown of glory
In the hand of the Lord,
And a royal diadem
In the hand of your God.
You shall no longer be termed Forsaken,
Nor shall your land any more be termed Desolate;
But you shall be called Hephzibah, and your land Beulah;
For the Lord delights in you,
And your land shall be married.

For as a young man marries a virgin,

So shall your sons marry you;

And as the bridegroom rejoices over the bride,

So shall your God rejoice over you.

I have set watchmen on your walls, O Jerusalem;

They shall never hold their peace day or night.

You who make mention of the Lord, do not keep silent,

And give Him no rest till He establishes

And till He makes Jerusalem a praise in the earth.

The Lord has sworn by His right hand And by the arm of His strength: "Surely I will no longer give your grain As food for your enemies; And the sons of the foreigner shall not drink your new wine, For which you have labored.

But those who have gathered it shall eat it,

And praise the Lord;

Those who have brought it together shall drink it in My holy courts." Go through, Go through the gates!

Prepare the way for the people;

Build up, Build up the highway! Take out the stones,

Lift up a banner for the peoples!

Indeed the Lord has proclaimed

To the end of the world:

"Say to the daughter of Zion,

'Surely your salvation is coming;

Behold, His reward is with Him,

And His work before Him.'"

And they shall call them The Holy People,

The Redeemed of the Lord;

And you shall be called Sought Out,

A City Not Forsaken."

Personal Prayer Of

- Thanksgiving, Praise and Worship,
- Repentance and Forgiveness of Sin,
- Empowerment by the Holy Spirit;
- Pleading and Activation of the power of the Blood of Jesus.

1. Hear, O my unrepentant enemies, and every stubborn pursuer of my destiny, by the fiery sword of the Spirit, receive reproach, insult and injury I strike a death blow to your satanic networks and alliances, in the mighty name of Jesus.

2. Abba, Father, cause everything, which You have not planted in the heavenlies be to uprooted, in the mighty name of Jesus.

3. Father, by a strong east wind drive away all the darkness that has surrounded our people, in the mighty name of Jesus. (be more specific.)

4. I release the manifestation of the full intensity of the Dayspring to shake the earth by the edges and shake out all the wicked structures in my life and our society, in the mighty name of Jesus.

5. I decree and declare that the sun shall not smite my life and my family in the day, or the moon by night. The Lord shall preserve us from all evil: He shall preserve our souls, in the mighty name of Jesus.

6. Father, dislodge the spiritual entities that are sitting at the gates to my divine heritage & inheritance, in the mighty name of Jesus.

7. Lord God, Lord of Hosts, throw into confusion all the chariots of hell, all the distractions and the spirit of deception that seeks to derail the progress of Your people, in the mighty name of Jesus (Exodus. 14:24).

8. Father, rescue my family from the hands of strange gods fighting against our breakthroughs and usher us into our divine destiny, in the mighty name of Jesus.

9. Father, help me to cast aside every cloak of ignorance, and put on Christ, to receive spiritual blessings, awakening and progress, in the mighty name of Jesus.

10. Abba Father, I pray that this time around, this ----------(family, country, etc) will see her Maker, and her children will know You, in the mighty name of Jesus.

11. Father, I desire, I hunger, and I thirst for a personal and intimate relationship with my Lord Jesus Christ.

12. Father, may the glory light of Jesus and the resurrection power of the Holy Spirit continue to shine brighter on my family and loved ones, in the mighty name of Jesus.

13. Abba Father, I pray that all the 7 Pillars in the Kingdom of God will begin to invade earth and fully function in my life, family, ministry, and our society, in Jesus' mighty name.

14. Abba Father, grant me the spirit of prayer to seek Your presence, and for the renewal of my mind and revival of my soul through the Word, in the mighty name of Jesus. (Ps. 19:7-11).

15. Abba Father, by the power of the Holy Spirit, I command and release peace and calm into every stormy situation in my life, and my family, finances, and my ministry, in the mighty name of Jesus. (Matt. 14:25)

16. May the resurrection power that raised Christ from the dead resurrect all my dead potentials, dreams and visions in realignment according to God's will, purpose, and plan for my life, in the mighty name of Jesus.

17. I invoke God's covenant of the Day and Night to speak and reveal knowledge that causes God to help and bless me, "With blessings of heaven above, Blessings of the deep that lies beneath,.." in the mighty name of Jesus. (Ps. 19:2, NIV; Genesis 49:25NKJV)

18. I therefore, declare restoration, the glory and the blessings of the Lord and His Prophetic Words upon my life, and family, in the mighty name of Jesus.

19. Father, I pray that the foundations of righteousness and justice will replace all other foundations of sin, iniquity in our families according to Your Word in 1 Corinthians 3:10-15; and Psalm 94:20; 97:2, in the mighty name of Jesus.

20. Abba Father, I thank You for the abundance and overflowing of Your spirit of life, grace, favor, and the opening of divine doors in my life, family, and ministry, in the mighty name of Jesus.

21. Abba Father, I thank You for Your visitation, presence, glory, and divine touch that has transformed my life and destiny forever; and from this day forth, I will never be the same again, in the mighty name of Jesus!

22. I speak healing and reconciliation of all things in the beginning of the new season in my life, my family, and our nation back to You Abba Father, according to Colossians 1:15-19, in the mighty name of Jesus.

23. I decree that no backlash of the enemy will come upon my life, family, nation and the body of Christ in the mighty name of Jesus.

24. Abba Father, I praise and extol You in this new season of time- for Thine is the Kingdom, the Power and the Glory, forever and ever, in the mighty name of Jesus. Amen.

"Be unceasing and persistent in prayer."

(1 Thessalonians 5:17 AMP)

CHAPTER 5

FIFTH WATCH (6:00 AM – 9:00 AM) EMPOWERMENT FOR MINISTRY

The Outpouring Of The Holy Spirit

FIRST WATCH OF THE DAYBREAK is between 6:00 am and 9:00 am that the Holy Spirit came in alignment with the. Hour of the manifested presence of the Holy Spirit on the day of Pentecost. Peter, on that day cautioned the crowd saying,

"These people are not drunk, as you suppose. It's only nine in the morning!"

(Acts 2:15NIV)

He then reminded them what God had spoken by the prophet Joel saying:

"In the last days, God says, I will pour out my Spirit on all people. Your sons and daughters will prophesy, your young men will see visions, your old men will dream dreams. Even on my servants, both men and women, I will pour out my Spirit in those days, and they will prophesy."

(Acts 2:17, 18 NIV).

- God gives the necessary equipment, resources, gifts, abilities, and opportunities for service and ministry.

When the people said "they were drunk" and Peter said "we are not drunk because it is just 9.00 in the morning," what was the implication? For those who have regular work schedules, people start work between the hours of 6.00 and 9.00 AM.

As you step out, ask God to equip you for the day, "Give us this day...." Thank God for the opportunity to work so that He can bless the work of your hands.

Time For Your Light To Shine This Day.

In Isaiah 60:1-2, it is written, "Arise, shine; For your light has come! And the glory of the Lord is risen upon you. For behold, the darkness shall cover the earth, And deep darkness the people; But the Lord will arise over you, And His glory will be seen upon you."

In Matthew 5:16, you are commanded to "Let your light so shine before men, that they may see your good works and glorify your Father in heaven."

- The spiritual significance of sunrise is having Jesus Christ the King of Kings and the Lord of Lords rise over us. As a king, decree and declare for it to be established!

Declaration And Utterances

"I will declare the decree:

The Lord has said to Me,
'You are My Son,
Today I have begotten You.
Ask of Me, and I will give You
The nations for Your inheritance,
And the ends of the earth for Your possession.
You shall break them with a rod of iron;
You shall dash them to pieces like a potter's vessel."

(Psalm 2:7-9NKJV)

Based on your authority in Psalm 2:7-9, instruct the sun as it rises over people, it should accurately represent Jesus Christ the Sun of righteousness and bring healings to the soul (i.e. the heart, emotion, mind), the body, and relationships, families, marriages, and also for the land.

Decree and declare that the sun of righteousness should rise with healing in its wings according to Malachi 4:2, so that there would be healing in your prayer life, health, relationships, family, nation, government, economy, etc.

FIFTH WATCH PRAYER POINTS
START PRAYING FROM 5:30 AM

Confession: Malachi 4:2, Acts 1:8, Acts 2:15, 17, 18

Malachi 4:2 NASB

"But for you who fear My name, the sun of righteousness will rise with healing in its wings; and you will go forth and skip about like calves from the stall."

Acts 1:8 NASB

"But you will receive power when the Holy Spirit has come upon you; and you shall be My witnesses both in Jerusalem, and in all Judea and Samaria, and even to the remotest part of the earth."

Acts 2:15, 17, 18 NIV

"… In the last days, God says, I will pour out my Spirit on all people. Your sons and daughters will prophesy, your young men will see visions, your old men will dream dreams. Even on my servants, both men and women, I will pour out my Spirit in those days, and they will prophesy."

Acts 10:38_NKJV

"How God anointed Jesus of Nazareth with the Holy Spirit and with power, who went about doing good and healing all who were oppressed by the devil, for God was with Him."

Personal Prayer Of

- Thanksgiving, Praise and Worship,
- Repentance and Forgiveness of Sin,
- Empowerment by the Holy Spirit;
- Pleading and Activation of the power of the Blood of Jesus.

1. I declare God's blessings of (strength, wisdom, power, provisions, healings, victory, glory...) and prophetic utterances through the Holy Spirit upon my life, family, church, city and nation in the mighty name of Jesus.

2. May the grace of God fall upon me that I may minister in humility, with blamelessness, faithful heart and undefiled eyes and lips, in the mighty name of Jesus.

3. Lord, baptize me with fire and with fresh anointing to labor in the Your vineyard and be most productive in the land, in the mighty name of Jesus.

4. I command the Dayspring to take hold of the morning and show the dawn its rightful place, its proper circuit and its divine purpose for my destiny, in the mighty name of Jesus. (Job 38:12).

5. Father, let my youth be renewed like the eagle's, in the mighty name of Jesus.

6. Abba Father, give us this day our daily bread in, the mighty name of Jesus.

7. Holy Spirit, breath of the Lord, fill my heart and strengthen my bones, in the mighty name of Jesus. (Job 32:7, 8; Isaiah 58:11)

8. God, may the Sun of Righteousness arise with healings in His wings in my prayer life, family, health, relationships, ministry, finances, and marriage, in Jesus' mighty name.

9. Father, may the power of Jesus empower Christians to willingly offer themselves for the labor of love in the vineyard of the Lord, in the mighty name of Jesus.

10. Father, may people everywhere willingly offer their bodies as instruments of righteousness, in the mighty name of Jesus. (Romans 6:13)

11. Father, transform our minds, strengthen our souls, and may all foundations of Satan in the Church be devoured, in the mighty name of Jesus. (Jer. 51:20-25)

12. Lord, release the Church for full employment in the service of God, in the mighty name of Jesus.

13. Lord, may the Church be established in God's rule in the land, in the mighty name of Jesus.

14. Father, release the manifestation of the full intensity of the Dayspring to shake the earth by the edges and shake out and uproot the wicked foundations and structures in the pillars of education in our nation, in Jesus' mighty name.

15. Father, Jehovah Nissi, You are our banner over our education system, in the mighty name of Jesus.

16. Abba, Father, raise up Your standards in the hearts of professionals, ministers, principals, teachers and workers in our education system, in the mighty name of Jesus.

17. Father, bless the students in this nation, that Your light and glory will shine upon them, in Jesus' mighty name.

18. Lord, come to this city in Your glory, so all the powers; principalities, and wicked spirits that torment the people will be chased out of town, in the mighty name of Jesus.

19. Lord of Hosts come and take hold of the gates of this nation and by the working of Your mighty strength, paralyze all the strongholds of the devil, in the mighty name of Jesus.

20. Father, enthrone Jesus in my family, church, school, neighborhood, city, state, and nation, in the mighty name of Jesus. (Psalm. 45:4; Psa. 74:12; Isa. 19:1)

21. Father, extend Your right hand and come to the defense of the poor and the needy in this city, state, and nation, in the mighty name of Jesus.

22. I speak healing and reconciliation of all things in the beginning of the new season in my life, my family, and the nation back to You Abba Father, according to Colossians 1:15-19, in the mighty name of Jesus.

23. I decree that no backlash of the enemy will come upon my life, family, nation and the body of Christ, in the mighty name of Jesus.

24. Abba Father, I praise and extol You in this new season of time- for Thine is the Kingdom, the Power and the Glory, forever and ever, in the mighty name of Jesus. Amen.

Having canceled out the certificate of debt consisting of legal demands [which were in force] against us and which were hostile to us. And this certificate He has set aside and completely removed by nailing it to the cross. When He had disarmed the rulers and authorities [those supernatural forces of evil operating against us], He made a public example of them [exhibiting them as captives in His triumphal procession], having triumphed over them through [c]the cross.

(Colossians 2:14-15 AMP)

CHAPTER 6

SIXTH WATCH (9:00 AM-12:00 NOON) TAP INTO THE CRUCIFIXION

Prepare For The Harvest.

THIS IS THE SECOND WATCH OF THE DAYBREAK OR THE THIRD HOUR of the day (i.e. 9.00 am)… In Matthew 20:2-3, it appears that one is considered idle if you've not started working by this time. As written,

"He agreed to pay them a denarius for the day and sent them into his vineyard. About nine in the morning he went out and saw others standing in the marketplace doing nothing."

- Just being busy with something doesn't necessarily give an assurance of any accomplishment in the eyes of God.
- Identify God's true purpose and His divine mandate for each moment of your life and pursue it.

Otherwise, you could find yourself wasting effort and energy like the prophets of Baal in 1 Kings 18:26-29, who after six hours of calling on their god were worse off bleeding and exhausted.

- Don't be consumed or preoccupied by earthly pursuits that do not advance or promote the divine agenda.

By 9.00 am, you should have started fulfilling the purpose for which you came to earth. How?

- Start by reading and meditating on the Word. Intercede for the Kingdom of Heaven to invade the earth on behalf of the saints!

This is the time to harvest prayers prayed at dawn. A time to harvest the promises of God, this is the time to expect the manifestation of God's promises for your life as in the case of David in 2 Samuel 7:25-29.

This is the watch to appropriate the promises of cleansing, a new heart, a new spirit, willingness to work, increase, and be fruitful, as contained in Ezekiel 36:25-38.

Pray For A Crucified Life.

To reap the harvest of the crucifixion, let us ask God to help us manifest all of the values of crucified life, by mortifying the deeds of our flesh as stated in Romans 8:12-15.

We are also commanded to,

"Put to death, therefore, whatever belongs to your earthly nature: sexual immorality, impurity, lust, evil desires and greed, which is idolatry."

(Colossians 3:5NIV)

Ask God to cleanse you of idolatry! (Anything you adore more than God is an idol)

According to Galatians 2:20,

"If we have been crucified with Christ, then we no longer live, but Christ lives in us. Therefore, the life we now live in the body, we live by faith in the Son of God, who loved us and gave himself for us."

- After a crucified life comes the time to put off the old man and put on the Lord Jesus Christ according to Colossians. 3:2-11.

This is the time to nail witchcraft, bitterness, jealousy, the spirit of anger, backbiting, gossip, slander, deception, lying, hypocrisy and in fact, all the properties and personality traits of the devil and all the works of the flesh to the Cross in line with Gal. 2:20, 5:19-21.

Appropriate The Benefits Of The Cross

(Healing, prosperity, forgiveness, strength, etc.). Jesus was crucified at the third hour (Mark 15:25, Matt. 27:45). After having been on the cross for three hours, darkness came upon the face of the earth at noon, and then at 3.00pm, He died and the period of darkness ended after enduring six hours on the Cross. The number six stands for human suffering! Did God work according to the watches of the day, especially pertaining to the crucifixion?

Forgiveness And Healing Of Relationships

A time to pray for forgiveness and the release of the offense of others! This is the best time to pray this portion of the model prayer the Lord Jesus

Christ taught His disciples in line with His intercession for our sins on the day of crucifixion saying:

"Father, forgive them; for they know not what they do."

(Luke 23:34)

"Forgive Us for our Trespasses… as We Forgive…"

(Matthew 6:12)

- In other words, it is time to pray for the healing of relationships, and also for the spiritual healing of diseases, sins, transgressions and iniquities. For in Isaiah, God says: "I, even I, am He who blots out your transgressions for My own sake; And I will not remember your sins.
- God is willing to cleanse us for His own sake!
- He will restore and bless us for His own sake!

In Ezekiel this is what God says to us,

"Then I will sprinkle clean water on you, and you shall be clean;
I will cleanse you from all your filthiness and from all your idols.
I will give you a new heart and put a new spirit within you;
I will take the heart of stone out of your flesh and give you a heart of flesh.
I will put My Spirit within you and cause you to walk in My statutes, and you will keep My judgments and do them. Then you shall dwell in the land that I gave to your fathers; you shall be My people, and I will be your God.
I will deliver you from all your uncleanliness.
I will call for the grain and multiply it, and bring no famine upon you.

And I will multiply the fruit of your trees and the increase of your fields, so that you need never again bear the reproach of famine among the nations.

Then you will remember your evil ways and your deeds that were not good; and you will loathe yourselves in your own sight, for your iniquities and your abominations.

Not for your sake do I do this," says the Lord God, "let it be known to you. Be ashamed and confounded for your own ways, O house of Israel!" 'Thus says the Lord God: "On the day that I cleanse you from all your iniquities,

I will also enable you to dwell in the cities, and the ruins shall be rebuilt. The desolate land shall be tilled instead of lying desolate in the sight of all who pass by. So they will say, 'This land that was desolate has become like the garden of Eden; and the wasted, desolate, and ruined cities are now fortified and inhabited.'

Then the nations which are left all around you shall know that I, the Lord, have rebuilt the ruined places and planted what was desolate.

I, the Lord, have spoken it, and I will do it."

(Ezekiel 36:25-36 NKJV)

SIXTH WATCH PRAYER POINTS
START PRAYING FROM 8:30 AM

Confession: Ps. 148, 2 Sam. 7:25-29, Jos. 23:14

2 Samuel 7:25-29 NKJV

"Now, O Lord God, the word which You have spoken concerning Your servant and concerning his house, establish it forever and do as You have said. So let Your name be magnified forever, saying, 'The Lord of hosts is the God over Israel.' And let the house of Your servant David be established before You. For You, O Lord of hosts, the God of Israel, have revealed this to Your servant, saying, 'I will build you a house.' Therefore Your servant has found it in his heart to pray this prayer to You. "And now, O Lord God, You are God, and Your Words are true, and You have promised this goodness to Your servant.

Now therefore, let it please You to bless the house of Your servant, that it may continue before You forever; for You, O Lord God, have spoken it, and with Your blessing let the house of Your servant be blessed forever."

Joshua 23:14 NKJV

"Behold, this day I am going the way of all the earth. And you know in all your hearts and in all your souls, that not one thing has failed of all the good things which the Lord your God spoke concerning you. All have come to pass for you; not one word of them has failed."

Personal Prayer Of

- Thanksgiving, Praise and Worship,
- Repentance and Forgiveness of Sin,
- Empowerment by the Holy Spirit;
- Pleading and Activation of the power of the Blood of Jesus.

1. Father God, baptize me with spiritual joy so I can give You continuous praise from my lips, in Jesus' mighty name.

2. Abba Father, pour Your grace on me and enable me to die to the flesh and the world so I can begin to live the crucified life of Christ according to John 12:24 and Galatians. 2:20, in the mighty name of Jesus.

3. I apply the benefit of the Cross to my life, family, marriage, job, finance, ministry, in the mighty name of Jesus.

4. God, fill the hearts of Your people with the spirit of forgiveness, and heal our broken relationships in our families, churches, communities and our situations, in the mighty name of Jesus.

5. May the healing power of the blood, and the broken body of Jesus, quicken and heal and dominate our lives, in the mighty name of Jesus.

6. Abba Father, I ask for, and receive Your grace to enable me to take my cross and follow Jesus, in Jesus' mighty name.

7. Lord God, baptized me with the humility of Jesus that I may always humble myself before You, as Jesus did on the Cross, in the mighty name of Jesus (Phil. 2:8-10).

8. Lord God, may all Christians carry the yoke of the Lord, even as they walk in meekness, and lowly heart, in the mighty name of Jesus.

9. Abba Father, by Your Holy Spirit, open up my spirit man to Your Word and help me to live in the Spirit and by the Spirit, in the mighty name of Jesus (Romans. 8:12-15).

10. Father, I lift up the voice of the Blood on behalf of my life, family and in all circumstances so I can operate in Your perfect will, in the mighty name of Jesus.

11. Father, cause all who are heavy laden and labor to look up to You for help, in the mighty name of Jesus.

12. Abba Father, by Your Holy Spirit grant me a clear vision of my life and ministry, in the mighty name of Jesus.

13. Lord, set all Christians free from every evil desire, in the mighty name of Jesus. (Col. 2:11, Gal. 2:20)

14. Holy Spirit, empower every Christian to experience the resurrection life of Christ Jesus, in the mighty name of Jesus (Colossians 3:1-4).

15. Father, covenant-keeping God, may Your promises to me be fulfilled in all areas of my life, in the mighty name of Jesus.

16. Lord, may the spirit of confusion and chaos, division and strife not prevail against Your children and Your church, in the mighty name of Jesus.

17. Abba Father, take hold of the pillar of science and technology in our nation and shake out any faulty, evil and wicked components that fights against Your Kingdom, in the mighty name of Jesus.

18. I break any evil covenant and associations binding me to the kingdom of darkness, in the mighty name of Jesus.

19. Holy Spirit, plant and build the foundations of justice, might, righteousness, excellence, knowledge, wisdom, understanding, and counsel, and surround me with Your wall of fire, in the mighty name of Jesus.

20. Father, in the mighty name of Jesus, I declare restoration, the glory and the blessings of THE LORD upon the 8 pillars of society, and the people of this land.

21. I release God's blessings, knowledge, wisdom, discoveries, wealth for the Church and our nation and prophetic words upon our science and technology, in Jesus' mighty name.

22. I speak healing and reconciliation of all things in the beginning of the new season in my life, my family, my nation back to You Abba, Father, according to Colossians 1:15-19, in the mighty name of Jesus.

23. I decree that no backlash of the enemy will come upon my life, family, nation and the body of Christ, in the mighty name of Jesus.

24. Abba Father, I praise and extol You in this new season of time- for Thine is the Kingdom, the Power and the Glory, forever and ever, in the mighty name of Jesus. Amen.

"Therefore confess your sins to each other and pray for each other so that you may be healed. The prayer of a righteous person is powerful and effective."

(James 5:16 NIV)

CHAPTER 7

SEVENTH WATCH (12:00 PM - 3:00 PM) SHAKE ALL FOUNDATIONS

Access The Secret Place Of The Most High.

THE SEVENTH WATCH OR THIRD WATCH OF THE DAYBREAK OR THE SIXTH HOUR OR THE FULLNESS OF DAY, is the watch that introduces the Midday, otherwise known as the Noon. (Psa. 55:17, Prov. 4:18, Isa. 58:10, Job 11:15, Psa. 37:3, Jer. 20:16).

Both the midday and the midnight are very important. Let us look at the Significance of this watch.

"It is the time to pray to dwell in the secret place of the Most High, abiding under the shadow of the Almighty, and making the Most High your habitation."

(Psalm 91:1)

- The midday can be dangerous!

God has commanded the sun to rule the daytime according to Genesis 1:16. And so the Psalmist prayed,

"The sun shall not strike you by day, nor the moon by night"

(Psalm 121:6)

"Nor of the pestilence that walks in darkness, nor of the destruction that lays waste at noonday"

(Psalm 91:6)

- The midday is the fullness of the day and it is the beginning of the Sixth hour.

"At midday, O king, along the road I saw a light from heaven, brighter than the sun, shining around me and those who journeyed with me."

(Acts 26:13, NKJV)

Deliverance From Evil Foundations

A time to take back the pillar of Media & the Entertainment industry from Satan the king of the power of the air; uproot its wicked foundations, bind the wicked spirits controlling and influencing it and return control to the righteous in our nation. How strong and firm are your ancestral foundations?

- If the foundation is destroyed, what, can the righteous do? (Psalm 11:3)
- Pray that your life would be brighter, without darkness and for your light to expose and expel all hidden satanic foundational agendas.

"It is also the time of exercising your God-given dominion, operating in love, receiving divine lift, and letting your light shine brighter until the full light of day is attained."

(Prov. 4:18)

This is a very important time to pray in line with Acts 10:9,

"The next day, as they went on their journey and drew near the city, Peter went up on the housetop to pray, about the sixth hour."

(i.e.: Noon time) This is the time that the sun is at its fullest and should yield its optimum best.

- Pray that the sun will yield its best and precious fruit to you, in line with Deuteronomy 33:13-14.

"Of Joseph he said, Blessed of the Lord be his land,
With the choice things of heaven, with the dew,
And from the deep lying beneath,
And with the choice yield of the sun,
And with the choice produce of the months."

Defeat, Destruction That Stalks At Noontime

This is the time to pray not to be led into any temptation, deception, enticement, trap, or snare of the enemy.

"Prepare war against her; Arise, and let us go up at noon. Woe to us, for the day goes away, For the shadows of the evening are lengthening. Arise, and let us go by night, And let us destroy her palaces."

(Jeremiah 6:4NKJV)

- Destruction is released at midday, according to Psalm 91:6.

- Pray and cut off all satanic arrows that are released at this time.

- This is the time to invoke God's Justice on your behalf (Psalm 92:6-7).

The destruction at this time will not get you, your family, church, ministry, job, finances, marriage, etc.

- Because we declare that the mystery of the secret place of the Most High would begin to speak on our behalf by the Blood of Jesus, the Lamb of God.

SEVENTH WATCH PRAYER POINTS START PRAYING FROM 11:30 AM

Confession: Psalm 148, Psalm 55:16-23, Proverbs 4:18, Isaiah 58:10

Psalm 55:16-23 NKJV

"As for me, I will call upon God, And the Lord shall save me.

Evening and morning and at noon I will pray, and cry aloud, And He shall hear my voice. He has redeemed my soul in peace from the battle that was against me, For there were many against me.

God will hear, and afflict them, Even He who abides from of old. Because they do not change, Therefore they do not fear God. He has put forth his hands against those who were at peace with him; He has broken his covenant.

The words of his mouth were smoother than butter, But war was in his heart; His words were softer than oil, Yet they were drawn swords.

Cast your burden on the Lord, And He shall sustain you; He shall never permit the righteous to be moved.

But You, O God, shall bring them down to the pit of destruction; Bloodthirsty and deceitful men shall not live out half their days; But I will trust in You."

Proverbs 4:18 NKJV

"But the path of the just is like the shining sun, That shines ever brighter unto the perfect day."

Isaiah 58:10 NKJV

"If you extend your soul to the hungry and satisfy the afflicted soul, then your light shall dawn in the darkness, and your darkness shall be as the noonday."

Personal Prayer Of

- Thanksgiving, Praise and Worship,
- Repentance and Forgiveness of Sin,
- Empowerment by the Holy Spirit;
- Pleading and Activation of the power of the Blood of Jesus.

1. Abba Father, grant me refuge and rest under Your everlasting wings, in the mighty name of Jesus.
2. God, deliver me from every terror of the night and every arrow that flies by day, in the mighty name of Jesus.
3. May the protection of the Lord become the portion of my household, in the mighty name of Jesus.
4. May my path shine even brighter till the fullness of the day, in the mighty name of Jesus (Prov. 4:18).
5. Every advantage of midday being used by the enemy of my soul to attack my destiny, BE CONVERTED into stumbling darkness now! In the mighty name of Jesus.
6. Abba Father, protect Your people from the pestilence that walks in darkness and the destruction that wastes at noonday according to Psalm 91:6, in Jesus' mighty name.

7. Wasting arrows of midday assigned to cause disaster against my family and I, we are not your candidate, RELOCATE BACK to your senders and WASTE THEM!!! In the mighty name of Jesus. (Psalm 91:6)

8. I command all satanic arrows present in my life, to lose their power, in the mighty name of Jesus.

9. The powers of my father's house, limiting my favor and divine benefits, I uproot you from your power-base by the blood of Jesus, BE DISGRACED AT NOONDAY AND BECOME DESOLATE BY FIRE!!! In the mighty name of Jesus. (Zephaniah 2:4)

10. Every power that attacked me in the night and is now celebrating at midday, it is payback time! I reverse your joy and terminate your victory; Somersault now and die as a victim of your own wickedness against me, in the mighty name of Jesus. (Deut. 28:29)

11. Abba Father, illuminate my horizon, and brighten my darkness, in the mighty name of Jesus.

12. May Christians all over the world invoke, activate, and experience the benefits of the blood of Jesus in their lives, in the mighty name of Jesus (Matt. 27:45-53).

13. Lord, rescue Your Church and its ministries in this nation and around the world from the plague that destroy at midday, in the mighty name of Jesus.

14. Father, instead of destruction, may there be the establishment of Your Will and Your purpose for the land, in the mighty name of Jesus.

15. Father, may the rays of Your powerful light introduce new ideas, new perceptions, new ways and methods of doing things from

Your Word into my life, family, Church, and land, in the mighty name of Jesus (Acts 9:1-6).

16. Father, lift up the light of Your countenance over the church so that her path of righteousness is like shining sun, shining ever brighter until the full light of the day, in the mighty name of Jesus. (Psalm 44:3, Prov. 4:18).

17. Abba Father, I pray that the shelter of the Most High will be the protective canopy covering of the church, especially in enemy territories, in the mighty name of Jesus (Psalm 91).

18. Abba Father, let there be a divine change in the media landscape of this nation, in the mighty name of Jesus.

19. Abba Father, Righteous Judge of the Universe, uproot the wicked foundations of the media and entertainment industry, in the land and bind the wicked spirits controlling and influencing them, in the mighty name of Jesus.

20. Abba Father, send the Archangel Michael to take back the pillar of Media & the Entertainment industry from Satan the king of the power of the air, and return control to the righteous in our nation, in the mighty name of Jesus.

21. I declare the Lord Jesus as the Jehovah Nissi over Media & Entertainment industry. Amen!

22. I speak healing and reconciliation of all things in the beginning of the new season in my life, my family, my nation back to You Abba Father, according to Colossians 1:15-19, in the mighty name of Jesus.

23. I decree that no backlash of the enemy will come upon my life, family, nation and the body of Christ, in the mighty name of Jesus.

24. Abba Father, I praise and extol You in this new season of time- for Thine is the Kingdom, the Power and the Glory, forever and ever, in the mighty name of Jesus. Amen

"Have you commanded the morning since your days began,
And caused the dawn to know its place,"

(Job 38:12 NKJV)

CHAPTER 8

EIGHTH WATCH (3:00 PM - 6:00 PM) THE HOUR OF PRAYER MIRACLES

Hour Of Victory, Access And Miracles

THE FOURTH WATCH OF THE DAYBREAK OR THE NINTH HOUR is the watch which begins at 3:00 pm and ushers in The Hour of Prayer or the "miracle hour" according to Acts 3:1, Acts 10:30

Now Peter and John went up together into the temple at the hour of prayer, being the ninth hour.

(Acts 3:1)

A vital characteristic, or practice that identifies the church, is Prayer. Jesus told the people,

"It is written, My house shall be called the house of prayer."

- Prayer is therefore, the most important privilege of the entire church. Prayer, is the only hour in the Bible that is specifically referred to as the Hour of Prayer which begins at 3:00 PM.

Time To Remove Limiting Factors

This was the time that the veil in front of the Holy of Holies was torn from top to bottom. (Luke 23:44-46) We have access to the Throne Room of Grace, to the Holy of Holies! This watch is therefore the time for access!

This time is also an hour when the work of the Cross was completed to usher:

- Revelation,
- Grace,
- Power,
- Glory,
- The voice of the Lord,
- Triumph, and the
- Removing of Veils (Luke 23:45-46),
- In our liberation.

This is the hour of the establishment of God's Judgment. Why? Righteousness and Justice are the foundation of God's Throne. (Psalm 89:14)

Justice was served at the Cross and Satan was defeated.

This is the time to die to the world (self). Remember, Jesus died in your place for you to receive the benefits of the Cross.

- This time is also the time of seeking the Lord in Truth.

You can therefore boldly say,

"I have been crucified with Christ; it is no longer I who live, but Christ lives in me; and the life which I now live in the flesh I live by faith in the Son of God, who loved me and gave Himself for me."

(Galatians 2:20, NKJV)

- Pray for **deliverance** during this watch.

Jesus went through six hours of suffering for the deliverance of humankind and the universe as written,

"Having wiped out the handwriting of requirements that was against us, which was contrary to us. And He has taken it out of the way, having nailed it to the cross. Having disarmed principalities and powers, He made a public spectacle of them, triumphing over them in it."

(Col. 2:14-15 NKJV).

At 3:00 pm Jesus gave up the ghost. When Jesus said, "It is finished!"

- This is the hour and the voice of triumph over sin, Satan, hell, and death.

He declared victory at Calvary as written,

"After this, Jesus, knowing that all things were now accomplished, that the Scripture might be fulfilled, said, "I thirst!"… So when Jesus had received the sour wine, He said, "It is finished!" And bowing His head, He gave up His spirit."

(John 19:28-30, NKJV)

- It is also the time for the miraculous and angelic visitation.

An angel was dispatched to Cornelius to invite Peter to reveal to him what he must know, receive, and do (ie: Who Jesus is, receive the gift of the Holy Spirit, and be baptized with water). Of the angelic visitation, Cornelius told Peter,

"Four days ago I was fasting until this hour; and at the ninth hour I prayed in my house, and, behold, a man stood before me in bright clothing, and said, 'Cornelius, your prayer has been heard, and your alms are remembered in the sight of God."

(Acts 10:31NKJV).

- This time is also the time of the evening sacrifice.

It was at this time that Elijah called forth fire from Heaven to consume the prophets of Baal on Mt. Carmel. (1 Kings 18:29, 30, 36-39)

Time To Change And Shape History

The Hour of Covenant: This was the time God changed history. This period is the hour of transformation. This watch happens to be the time that Jesus gave up the ghost with a loud voice. When Jesus gave up the ghost, the greatest legal contract in history was established forever because:

- He now established a covenant for us with God and there was a triumphant Glory over hell, death and the grave,

The Bible says at that hour, darkness departed. As written, "The covering of darkness cast over this nation shall be broken! Pray Isaiah 60:1-2; Psalm 29.

In Matthew we read.

"And about the ninth hour Jesus cried with a loud voice, saying, Eli, Eli, lama sabachthani? That is to say, My God, my God, why hast thou forsaken me?"

(Matthew 27:46)

This is because the Father turned His back on sin which Jesus carried on our behalf.

- We must pray that the Church in this nation will turn her back on sin; so that leadership in family, government, church, economy, etc. will also turn their back on sin.

Possess this gate of the day, just like in the other Watches not only for yourself, but also for your family, your neighborhood, community, the city, the nation, and the church, so that God's Kingdom will prevail and advance in this generation!

EIGHTH WATCH PRAYER POINTS
START PRAYING FROM 2:30 PM

Confession: Psalm 148, Psa. 29, Luke 23:44-46, Zech. 18-21, Isa.17:12-14,

Luke 23:44-46

"And it was about the sixth hour, and there was darkness over all the earth until the ninth hour. And the sun was darkened, and the veil of the temple was rent in the midst. And when Jesus had cried with a loud voice, ... he gave up the ghost."

Zechariah 18-21

"Then I looked up, and there before me were four horns. I asked the angel who was speaking to me, "What are these?" He answered me, "These are the horns that scattered Judah, Israel and Jerusalem." Then the Lord showed me four craftsmen. I asked, "What are these coming to do?" He answered, "These are the horns that scattered Judah so that no one could raise their head, but the craftsmen have come to terrify them and throw down these horns of the nations who lifted up their horns against the land of Judah to scatter its people."

Isaiah17: 12-14

"Woe to the multitude of many people, ... but God shall rebuke them, and they shall flee far off, and shall be chased as the chaff of the mountains before the wind, and like a rolling thing before the whirlwind. And behold at eveningtide trouble; and before the morning he is not. This is the portion of them that spoil us, and ... rob us."

Personal Prayer Of

- Thanksgiving, Praise and Worship,
- Repentance and Forgiveness of Sin,
- Empowerment by the Holy Spirit;
- Pleading and Activation of the power of the Blood of Jesus.

1. Lord, remove every obstacle and hindrance from my heart and mind and free me to seek You, and call upon You as a good son relates to his Father, in Jesus' mighty name.

2. God, I pray that You will redeem our spiritual sight of all the things that have blindfolded us from seeing visions from You, in the mighty name of Jesus (Isa. 44:17-18).

3. God, clear my heart and mind of filth and spiritual bondage and set me at liberty to receive divine dreams, revelations and insight from the Holy Spirit, in the mighty name of Jesus (Acts 10:10-11).

4. Abba Father, I thank You for the voice of triumph, and of the Blood at this hour, in the mighty name of Jesus.

5. Father, I pray that everyone in my family will have an encounter with You that will usher them into their place in Christ, in life, in this generation and in this season, in the mighty name of Jesus Christ of Nazareth.

6. Lord, help me put to death the works of the flesh and not live according to its sinful nature but rather live according to the spirit, in Jesus' mighty name.

7. Abba, Father, in the same way You turned Your back on Your Son because of sin, I pray for divine help so I can thoroughly turn my back on sin and every dealing with the 'old man' or anything of the flesh, in Jesus' mighty name.

8. God, I pray that You deal with all demonic transactions in our hearts, minds, emotions, wills and bodies; that distracts us from focusing on Your Will, purposes, and plans, in the mighty name of Jesus (Matthew. 21:12).

9. Father, I pray that Jesus will find me ready when He comes for His church, in the mighty name of Jesus.

10. Lord, grant me the wisdom to put oil in my lamp, and even hold some in reserve, so I will have the stamina to wait for You, in the mighty name of Jesus (Lk. 12:38, 35).

11. God, raise Christians who will eagerly watch and pray so that Your purpose and Will, be established in the land, in the mighty name of Jesus (Luke 12:35; Isa. 62:6-7).

12. God, I pray that You baptize every Christian with hatred for sin in our generation, in the mighty name of Jesus (Hebrew. 12:1-2).

13. Abba Father, I pray that You send Your angels to help Christians take off every garment of besetting sin of lust, pride, bitterness, anger, laziness, sexual immorality, in the mighty name of Jesus Christ of Nazareth. (Zechariah. 3:1, Colossians. 3:1-5, Hebrew. 12:1).

14. Father, deliver Your people from fighting all unnecessary battles, instead of those by divine appointment, in the mighty name of Jesus (1 Samuel. 17:40-58).

15. Abba Father, I pray that You pull down every wall of division and personal ambitions in the body of Christ, in the mighty name of Jesus (Acts 10:23-35).

16. Father, I pray that the people of this nation in their generation will forsake their wicked ways and turn to You, in the mighty name of Jesus (Isaiah. 55:6-7).

17. Father, remove every veil of darkness from peoples' minds so that they can comprehend Your Will, plan and purposes for their generation, in Jesus' mighty name.

18. The power of God, break the activities of the devil on this continent and let liberty be proclaimed to all, from young to old, children to adults, male and female, the rich and the poor, in the mighty name of Jesus (Matt. 27:51-52).

19. I pray and activate the blood of Jesus to destroy all satanic covenants with the grave, holding our buried economic resources, and potentials, and cause them to be released for the prosperity of our nation, in the mighty name of Jesus (Isaiah. 28:14-18).

20. Lord, come to this city in Your glory, so all the powers; principalities and wicked spirits that torment the people will be chased out of town, in Jesus' mighty name. (Exodus. 11:4)

21. I speak healing and reconciliation of all things in the beginning of the new season in my life, my family, my nation, and the church back to You Abba, Father, according to Colossians 1:15-19, in Jesus' mighty name.

22. I'm more than a conqueror. I decree that no backlash of the enemy will come upon my life, family, nation and the body of Christ, in the mighty name of Jesus.

23. Abba Father, I praise and extol You in this new season of time- for Thine is the Kingdom, the Power and the Glory, forever and ever, in the mighty name of Jesus. Amen

24. I seal theses prayers with the blood of Jesus and the firepower of the Holy Spirit, and I stand on the Word of God in Luke 1:37,

that with God nothing shall be impossible, indeed with God all things are possible, in the mighty name of Jesus.

APPENDIX A

ORGANIZING A CORPORATE PRAYER WATCH

"I have set watchmen on your walls, O Jerusalem; they shall never hold their peace day or night. You who make mention of the Lord, do not keep silent, and give Him no rest till He establishes and till He makes Jerusalem a praise in the earth."

(Isaiah. 62:6-7NKJV)

The secret of effective warfare lies in sneak nighttime attacks on unsuspecting targets. The enemy uses this strategy to steal, kill, and destroy those who are unwilling to pay the price for maintaining night vigils over their kingdom and palaces.

According to Jesus,

"When a strong man, fully armed, guards his own palace, his goods are in peace. But when a stronger than he comes upon him and overcomes him, he takes from him all his armor in which he trusted, and divides his spoils."

(Luke 11:21-22 NKJV)

Fear Not! By the Word, and by prayer; King Jesus, the King of Kings, and the Lord of Lords, has your back and victory!

It bears repeating that we need to harness our spiritual muscles by letting these prayers be part of our daily spiritual exercises. However, for your prayers to be effective, seek the presence of God, live a holy and righteous life, repent and confess all your sins, including the transgressions and the iniquities of your bloodline, forgive others who have wronged you, stay above offense and not give room to the devil to harass, oppress, and suppress you, and your loved ones.

During a prayer watch, the emphasis is on nightly:

- "watchful attention, or sensitivity" to
- the level of heightened spiritual activities of evil
- in the realms and
- the atmospheres
- of a location.

We are commanded to watch and pray and seek God as written,

"Arise, cry out in the night, as the watches of the night begin; pour out your heart like water in the presence of the Lord. Lift up your hands to him for the lives of your children, who faint from hunger at every street corner."

(Lamentation 2:18-19)

Also in Psalms 119:148, we read,

"My eyes stay open through the watches of the night that I may meditate on your promises."

God expects His people individually and corporately to exercise dominion over evil, whether spirits, or men, and also the forces of nature. God expects His children to take their rightful position and begin to rule. As written,

"Thou madest him to have dominion over the works of thy hands; thou hast put all things under his feet."

(Psalms 8:6)

I. Purpose of a Corporate Prayer Watch

The bible says,

"Two are better than one, for they have a good reward for their efforts."

(Ecclesiastes 4:9)

By prayer watches we pull together our prayer power to build and expand our ministries through the wisdom and counsel of heaven to:

1. Provide ongoing prayer coverage for cities and regions in preparation for revival. (Isaiah 62:1)
2. Promote unity and networking between churches in the community through prayer and relationships. (Matthew 22:37-40)
3. Develop strategic level prayer initiatives for the region in cooperation with state and national leadership. (Ezekiel 4:1-2).

121

4. Help raise the spiritual climate of deliverance and revival over the region by meeting regularly in focused strategic prayer sessions. In James 5:16,

- **Effectual** means: Producing desired results.
- **Fervent** means: Boiling hot.

II. Important Principles to Follow in Developing a Healthy City /Regional Prayer Watch

1. Commit to a block of time each week to pray for the region, city church, family, school, community, or neighborhood. (James 4:8, 5:16) It is recommended that each person have their own personal time with the Lord during the week so that they can contribute more strategically based on their time constraints.

2. Apply the following rules for corporate prayer
   - Be of one accord, and in the bond of peace, and the unity of the Spirit.
   - Come ready and willing to participate by laying aside personal concerns and agendas. Avoid distractions!
   - Ask the Lord for and receive, and release grace to all involved in the corporate prayer watch.
   - Be consistent.
   - Be of one mind and of one accord
   - Be fervent.
   - Be persistent and don't give up.
   - Expect God to move on your behalf.

3. Always Start A Corporate Watch By Praying A Blessing
   - The blessing can be easily done by having participants pray a blessing for each other. Personal ministry can occur during this time.
   - Imparting a blessing is an important act of worship where people come under the canopy of the Kingdom of God.

1. Use testimony time to encourage faith and sharing of answered prayers as sacrifices of Thanksgiving, Praise, and as an act of Worship.
2. Persevere in keeping an atmosphere of grace and thanksgiving in the corporate setting, so that warfare can be effectual and a critical spirit kept from developing. (Heb. 4:16)
3. Focus on the Lord through worship and intercession in one accord, in sensitivity to the leading of the Holy Spirit (John 6:13)
4. Focus on heavenly things and not on yourself or men.
5. Don't' take offense
6. Don't stress yourself. Relax your mind.
7. Be an active participant and not a bystander.
8. Receive, accept, and enjoy the presence of the Lord.

III. Keep Strategies Simple So That Prayer Can Be Sustained For The Long Haul.

1. Small groups can gain much by dividing the watch to allow watchmen to take different hours at night/day each week to pray.
2. In order to sustain Kingdom advances made in the spiritual climate over your city/region, after the watch, it is recommended you commit to corporate gatherings on a consistent weekly basis.

3. Encourage periodic corporate "soaking" times of extended worship and intercession, i.e. 12, 24, 48 hours.

Keep Prayer Short and Simple

Since your ultimate goal is to persist and persevere in prayer, keep your prayer time simple. To this end:

- It is recommended that you pray for about 20 - 30 minutes over the gate of time, i.e. starting at least 10-15 minutes before the Hour, and then 10 -15 minutes after the Hour gate. Pray scriptures over the gates.

- Although the prayers are geared toward taking back our neighborhood, cities, and nation, they may be personalized to include praying for yourself and your loved ones as well. When you pray, a prayer point for your church, nation, etc., repeat it; mention the names of your loved ones, and also pray for them.

As You End Each Gate Of The Prayer Watch:

- Speak healing and reconciliation of all things in the beginning of the new season in your life, your nation, back to God (Colossians 1:15-19)

- Pray that no backlash of the enemy will come upon your life, family, your nation, and the body of Christ.

- Reconcile all things to God in this new season in your life, in your nation.

- Praise and extol the Lord God in this new season of time- finish by declaring "for Thine is the Kingdom, the Power and the Glory, forever and ever." Amen

Source:

Culled from:

Susan and Fred Rowe of California Prayer Watch for an effective prayer watch.

Jesus Is Lord Ministries:

http://jesusislordministries.in/Downloads/PrayeractivityattheWatches.pdf

APPENDIX B

COMMANDING YOUR EVENINGS

Abba Father, on this brand-new day (Date),

1. I thank You for granting me access to Mount Zion,
2. and unto the city of the living God,
3. the heavenly Jerusalem,
4. and to an innumerable company of angels,
5. To the general assembly
6. and church of the firstborn, which are written in heaven,
7. and to You Father, God,
8. the Judge of all,
9. and to the spirits of just men made perfect,
10. And to Jesus the mediator of the new covenant,
11. and to the blood of sprinkling,
12. that speaketh better things than that of Abel. (Hebrews 12:22-24 KJV)

Give ear, O heavens, and I will speak; hear, O earth, O ye lands and O ye seas, rivers and waters, mountains, hills, valleys, lowlands, plains, deserts, forest and High Places, O ye cities, states, and nations, governmental and financial institutions, law enforcement and order, jobs, employments, and the media, the words of God in my mouth and obey, in the mighty name of Jesus Christ of Nazareth.

O ye mighty angels who harken to the voice and do the bidding of the Most High God, I release you to bring to fruition swiftly, the utterances of His words in my mouth, in the mighty name of Jesus Christ of Nazareth.

GRACE

Abba Father, Father of all grace, on this brand-new day, I come to You and I ask for, and I receive and I accept Your:

1. Amazing grace,
2. Great grace,
3. Bounteous grace
4. Superabundant grace,
5. Overwhelming grace
6. Exceeding riches of Your grace
7. Grace upon grace and
8. The gift of righteousness

Based on Your word in Ephesians 2:7 and Romans 5:17 upon myself and family, in the mighty name of Jesus Christ of Nazareth.

LOVE

Father, I envelop myself and family in Your:

1. Sweet Tender-loving kindness love
2. Amazing love
3. Wonderous
4. Agape love
5. Calvary love
6. Steadfast love
7. Unfailing love
8. Faithful love
9. Compelling love
10. Manifested love
11. Demonstrated love
12. Encouraging love
13. Empowering love
14. Irresistible love
15. Can-do love
16. Immeasurable love
17. Unconditional love and
18. Everlasting love by which You have drawn me and my family into the eternal kingdom of Your Dear Son, my Lord Jesus Christ, according to Your word in Jeremiah 31:3 in the mighty name of Jesus.

HOLY SPIRIT

Father, I welcome the:

1. Sweet Fellowship
2. Indwelling
3. Infilling

4. Ability to live in, live with, live by, live for, live through and walk in the Spirit

5. Fresh Anointing

6. Divine Unction

7. Baptism of Fire

8. Prophetic and Apostolic Mantles of Fire

9. Chariots and Horses of Fire (2 Kings 6:17/Isaiah 66:15)

10. Prayer Mantle of Fire

11. Overshadowing of Your Spirit

12. Outpouring of Your Spirit based on Isaiah 44:3/Joel 2:28/Acts 2:17 upon myself and my seed.

Holy Spirit, as the deer pants after water, so my soul pants after Thee. Holy Spirit, I need You, I desire, I yearn for Your Presence. Father, I hunger and thirst after the Holy Spirit, therefore, Papa, pour a full measure of Your Spirit upon me and upon my seed; Father, pour Your Spirit upon us like flood on a dry ground, and bless my seed's seed, in the mighty name of Jesus Christ of Nazareth. Amen!!!

THE WHOLE ARMOR OF GOD

Father, in the name of Jesus and by the power of the Holy Spirit,

1. I put on the whole armor of God:

2. Father, let Your shield of light surround us;

3. Father, let Your strong banner represent us;

4. Father, You are our strong tower to protect and guard us;

5. Father, surround us with Your wall of fire;

6. Father, let Your mighty angels encamp around us;

7. Father, with the Blood of Jesus, I draw a circle line of protection around
   a. Myself and family
   b. Prayer family
   c. Church family,
   d. All those I have been interceding for and on
   e. All our possessions.

AGREE WITH THE WORD

Father, I connect my spirit to Your word in Colossians 2:13-15, and because the enemy was judged when Jesus went to the Cross, I ask You to avenge me of my adversary according to Your word in Luke 18:1-8, in the mighty name of Jesus.

Abba Father, let Your written judgments against the adversary be executed upon my enemies, in the mighty name of Jesus Christ of Nazareth.

Abba Father, by the testimony of the Blood of Jesus, silence the enemy, my adversaries, and all my accusers who have summoned me to Your courtroom, in the mighty name of Jesus Christ of Nazareth.

Father, I stand on Your word in Psalm 149:9, and I rebuke Satan and his kingdom of darkness warring against me and my family, in the mighty name of Jesus Christ of Nazareth.

I rebuke the spirit of poverty, of lack, insufficiency, barrenness, unfruitfulness, powerlessness, disgrace, dishonor, failure, rejection, curses, fear, anxiety, suppression, oppression, depression, disappointment, discouragement, and of death, in the mighty name of Jesus.

Father, with the voices of the adversary silenced, let revelations break forth, let healing break forth, let prosperity break forth, let the superabundant life break forth, let signs and wonders, and miracles break forth, in the mighty name of Jesus Christ of Nazareth!

Father, I agree and concur with the testimony and voices of heaven according to Your word in Hebrews 12:22-24 concerning my destiny based on the blood, and the finished work of the Cross, in the mighty name of Jesus.

THANKSGIVING FOR THE WORD

It is written,

"As for God, His way is perfect; The word of the Lord is proven; He is a shield to all who trust in Him."

(Psalm 18:30NKJV)

Father, I thank You for Your word, for:

1. Your word is life and alive.
2. Your word is true and faithful.
3. Your word is pure.
4. Your word is powerful and supreme.
5. By Your word, You made heaven and earth.
6. Your word is a lamp and a light for my path.
7. Your word is fire and hammer.
8. Your word is sharper than any two-edged sword.
9. You watch Your word to back it up. (Jer. 1:12)

10. Your word does not return to You void and empty-handed, but always accomplishes the purpose for which You sent it. (Isa. 55:11)

11. Your word is exalted above Your name. (Psalm 138:2)

12. Your word is everlasting: Even though the heaven and the earth pass away, Your word abides forever. (Matthew 24:35)

13. You have put Your word in my mouth and in my heart.

14. You will perform Your word concerning me.

THANKSGIVING FOR YOUR INHERITANCE

1. Father, I thank You that You created me in Your image and likeness.

2. Father, I came from You, I belong to You and You are my blood covenant partner.

3. Father, I thank You that I'm Your child, according to the Holy Spirit, in Romans 8:14-17.

4. I decree and declare that I am a child of God; (Gal. 4:7)

5. By the Spirit of adoption, I can call God, Abba Father.

6. I am an heir of God, and in fact, joint heirs with my Lord Jesus Christ.

7. Father, I thank You that by the blood of Jesus, You have made me a king and a priest to reign on earth.

8. Father, I thank You that it's Your pleasure to give me the kingdom. I have a godly heritage!

Father, I thank You that in Your discourse with our patriarch Abraham and his inheritance, You show us that:

1. Slaves do not receive an inheritance,

2. Servants do not receive an inheritance,

3. Workers do not receive an inheritance,

4. Officers do not receive an inheritance,

5. Even friends do not receive an inheritance,

6. Strangers definitely, do not receive an inheritance,

7. Only sons and daughters receive an inheritance.

INVOKE, ACTIVATE YOUR INHERITANCE

Father, I thank You that my Lord Jesus died so that by His death and covenanted blood, I can receive my inheritance from You. Abba Father, because:

1. You are A Consuming Fire, Father change my DNA into fire.

2. You are Light, Father, change my DNA into light.

3. You are My Creator, Father, let the creative genes in me become activated with signs and wonders.

4. You are Wind, let Your breath of life flow through me,

5. You are Spirit, energize and empower my spirit-man

Father, because I have spoken these words, let Your words in my mouth become fire and light according to Jeremiah 5:14. Father, let the fire of Your presence in my mouth consume my adversaries and those who seek to:

1. Collude and connive,

2. Condone, and Conspire

3. Contempt and Confuse,

4. Tempt and Trap

5. Distract and Discourage,

6. Disgrace and dishonor

7. Desecrate and Defile
8. Destroy and Kill
9. Discredit and Disqualify
10. Deny, me and my family from receiving and enjoying what You have given us.

Father, as I begin to give thanks, praise, and worship You, let the presence of Your fire in my mouth consume their devices, their evil merchandise of trade and of hatred, manipulation, and destruction; let them backfire upon their covens, satanic networks, associations and alliances, in the mighty name of Jesus Christ of Nazareth. Amen!

SEAL YOUR PRAYERS DECREES AND DECLARATIONS

Abba Father, according to Your word in Psalm 19:14, let the words of my mouth and the meditation of my heart Be acceptable in Your sight, O Lord, my strength and my Redeemer, in the mighty name of Jesus.

Father, I seal these prayers, decrees and declarations with the blood of Jesus and the fire of the Holy Spirit, in the mighty name of Jesus Christ of Nazareth!!! Amen!!!

APPENDIX C

BIBLE VERSES

Psalm 148 NIV

"Praise the Lord!

Praise the Lord from the heavens;

Praise Him in the heights!

^{2} Praise Him, all His angels;

Praise Him, all His hosts!

^{3} Praise Him, sun and moon;

Praise Him, all you stars of light!

^{4} Praise Him, you heavens of heavens,

And you waters above the heavens!

^{5} Let them praise the name of the Lord,

For He commanded and they were created.

^{6} He also established them forever and ever;

He made a decree which shall not pass away.

^{7} Praise the Lord from the earth,

You great sea creatures and all the depths;

^{8} Fire and hail, snow and clouds;

Stormy wind, fulfilling His word;

⁹ Mountains and all hills;

Fruitful trees and all cedars;

¹⁰ Beasts and all cattle;

Creeping things and flying fowl;

¹¹ Kings of the earth and all peoples;

Princes and all judges of the earth;

¹² Both young men and maidens;

Old men and children.

¹³ Let them praise the name of the Lord,

For His name alone is exalted;

His glory is above the earth and heaven.

¹⁴ And He has exalted the horn of His people,

The praise of all His saints-

Of the children of Israel,

A people near to Him.

Praise the Lord."

Psalm 59 KJV

"Deliver me from my enemies, O my God; Defend me from those who rise up against me. Deliver me from the workers of iniquity, And save me from bloodthirsty men. For look, they lie in wait for my life; The mighty gather against me, Not for my transgression nor for my sin, O Lord. They run and prepare themselves through no fault of mine. Awake to help me, and behold! You therefore, O Lord God of hosts, the God of Israel, Awake to punish all the nations; Do not be merciful to any wicked transgressors. Selah. At evening they return, They growl like a dog, And go all around the city. Indeed, they belch with their mouth; Swords are in their lips; For they say, "Who hears?" But You, O Lord, shall laugh at them; You shall have all the nations in derision. I will wait for You, O You his Strength; For God is my defense. My God of mercy shall come to meet me; God shall let me see my desire on my enemies. Do not slay them, lest my people forget; Scatter them by Your power, And bring them down, O Lord our shield. For the sin of their mouth and the words of their lips, Let them even be taken in their pride, And for the cursing and lying which they speak. Consume them in wrath, consume them, That they may not be; And let them know that God rules in Jacob To the ends of the earth. Selah

And at evening they return, They growl like a dog, And go all around the city. They wander up and down for food, And how if they are not satisfied. But I will sing of Your power; Yes, I will sing aloud of Your mercy in the morning; For You have been my defense And refuge in the day of my trouble.

To You, O my Strength, I will sing praises; For God is my defense, My God of mercy."

Psalm 29 NKJV
"Give unto the Lord, O you mighty ones,
Give unto the Lord glory and strength.
Give unto the Lord the glory due to His name;
Worship the Lord in the beauty of holiness.
The voice of the Lord is over the waters; The God of glory thunders; The Lord is over many waters.
The voice of the Lord is powerful;
The voice of the Lord is full of majesty.
The voice of the Lord breaks the cedars,
Yes, the Lord splinters the cedars of Lebanon.

He makes them also skip like a calf, Lebanon and Sirion like a young wild ox.

The voice of the Lord divides the flames of fire.

The voice of the Lord shakes the wilderness;

The Lord shakes the Wilderness of Kadesh.

The voice of the Lord makes the deer give birth,

And strips the forests bare;

And in His temple everyone says, "Glory!"

The Lord sat enthroned at the Flood, And the Lord sits as King forever.

The Lord will give strength to His people; The Lord will bless His people with peace."

Daniel 9:5-19 NKJV

"We have sinned and committed iniquity, we have done wickedly and rebelled, even by departing from Your precepts and Your judgments. Neither have we heeded Your servants the prophets, who spoke in Your name to our kings and our princes, to our fathers and all the people of the land. O Lord, righteousness belongs to You, but to us shame of face, as it is this day-to the men of Judah, to the inhabitants of Jerusalem and all Israel, those near and those far off in all the countries to which You have driven them, because of the unfaithfulness which they have committed against You.

"O Lord, to us belongs shame of face, to our kings, our princes, and our fathers, because we have sinned against You. To the Lord our God belong mercy and forgiveness, though we have rebelled against Him. We have not obeyed the voice of the Lord our God, to walk in His laws, which He set before us by His servants the prophets. Yes, all Israel has transgressed Your law, and has departed so as not to obey Your voice; therefore the curse and the oath written in the Law of Moses the servant of God have been poured out on us, because we have sinned against Him. And He has confirmed His words, which He spoke against us and against our judges who judged us, by bringing upon us a great disaster; for under the whole heaven such has never been done as what has been done to Jerusalem.

"As it is written in the Law of Moses, all this disaster has come upon us; yet we have not made our prayer before the Lord our God, that we might turn from our iniquities and understand Your truth. Therefore the Lord has kept the disaster in mind, and brought it upon us; for the Lord our God is righteous in all the works which He does, though we have not obeyed His voice. And now, O Lord our God, who brought Your people out of the land of Egypt with a mighty hand, and made Yourself a name, as it is this day-we have sinned, we have done wickedly!

[16] "O Lord, according to all Your righteousness, I pray, let Your anger and Your fury be turned away from Your city Jerusalem, Your holy mountain; because for our sins, and for the iniquities of our fathers, Jerusalem and Your people are a reproach to all those around us. [17] Now therefore, our God, hear the prayer of Your servant, and his supplications, and for the Lord's sake cause Your face to shine on Your sanctuary, which is desolate. [18] O my God, incline Your ear and hear; open Your eyes and see our desolations, and the city which is called by Your name; for we do not present our supplications before You because of our righteous deeds, but because of Your great mercies. O Lord, hear! O Lord, forgive! O Lord, listen and act! Do not delay for Your own sake, my God, for Your city and Your people are called by Your name."

Psalm 51 NKJV

"Have mercy upon me, O God,

According to Your lovingkindness;

According to the multitude of Your tender mercies,

Blot out my transgressions.

Wash me thoroughly from my iniquity,

And cleanse me from my sin.

For I acknowledge my transgressions,

And my sin is always before me.

Against You, You only, have I sinned,

And done this evil in Your sight-

That You may be found just when You speak,

And blameless when You judge.

Behold, I was brought forth in iniquity,

And in sin my mother conceived me. Behold, You desire truth in the inward parts,

And in the hidden part You will make me to know wisdom.

Purge me with hyssop, and I shall be clean;

Wash me, and I shall be whiter than snow.

Make me hear joy and gladness,

That the bones You have broken may rejoice.

Hide Your face from my sins,

And blot out all my iniquities.

Create in me a clean heart, O God,

And renew a steadfast spirit within me.

Do not cast me away from Your presence,

And do not take Your Holy Spirit from me.

Restore to me the joy of Your salvation,

And uphold me by Your generous Spirit.

Then I will teach transgressors Your ways,

And sinners shall be converted to You.

Deliver me from the guilt of bloodshed, O God,

The God of my salvation,

And my tongue shall sing aloud of Your righteousness.

O Lord, open my lips,

And my mouth shall show forth Your praise.

For You do not desire sacrifice, or else I would give it;

You do not delight in burnt offering.

The sacrifices of God are a broken spirit,

A broken and a contrite heart-

These, O God, You will not despise.

Do good in Your good pleasure to Zion;

Build the walls of Jerusalem.

Then You shall be pleased with the sacrifices of righteousness,

With burnt offering and whole burnt offering;

Then they shall offer bulls on Your altar."

Psalm 18:29-50 NKJV

"For by You I can run against a troop,

By my God I can leap over a wall.

[30] As for God, His way is perfect;

The word of the Lord is proven;

He is a shield to all who trust in Him.

[31] For who is God, except the Lord? And who is a rock, except our God?

[32] It is God who arms me with strength,

And makes my way perfect.

[33] He makes my feet like the feet of deer, And sets me on my high places.

[34] He teaches my hands to make war, So that my arms can bend a bow of bronze.

[35] You have also given me the shield of Your salvation; Your right hand has held me up,

Your gentleness has made me great.

[36] You enlarged my path under me, So my feet did not slip.

[37] I have pursued my enemies and overtaken them;

Neither did I turn back again till they were destroyed.

[38] I have wounded them, So that they could not rise;

They have fallen under my feet.

[39] For You have armed me with strength for the battle;

You have subdued under me those who rose up against me.

[40] You have also given me the necks of my enemies,

So that I destroyed those who hated me.

[41] They cried out, but there was none to save;

Even to the Lord, but He did not answer them.

[42] Then I beat them as fine as the dust before the wind;

I cast them out like dirt in the streets.

[43] You have delivered me from the strivings of the people;

You have made me the head of the nations;

A people I have not known shall serve me.

[44] As soon as they hear of me they obey me;

The foreigners submit to me.

[45] The foreigners fade away,

And come frightened from their hideouts.

[46] The Lord lives! Blessed be my Rock!

Let the God of my salvation be exalted.

[47] It is God who avenges me, And subdues the peoples under me;

[48] He delivers me from my enemies.

You also lift me up above those who rise against me;

You have delivered me from the violent man.

[49] Therefore I will give thanks to You, O Lord, among the Gentiles, And sing praises to Your name.

[50] Great deliverance He gives to His king, And shows mercy to His anointed, To David and his descendants forevermore."

REFERENCES

Source: "The 8 Prayer Watches," National Prayer Watch,
http://diasporaxchange.net/nationalprayerwatch/the_8_prayer_watches/
(Accessed September 3, 2011).

Susan and Fred Rowe California Prayer Watch:
http://diasporaxchange.net/nationalprayerwatch/contributions/249.pd
http://jesusislordministries.in/Downloads/PrayeractivityattheWatches.pdf
(Jesus Is Lord Ministries. Accessed August 12, 2014)

https://christonline.wordpress.com/2009/02/05/sexual-lusts-effects-of-masturbation-
porn-fornication-and-adultery/#comment-40089
(Accessed June 2, 2017)

Olukoya, D. K. Dr.; Prayer Rain. Lagos, Nigeria. Mountain of Fire and Miracles
Ministries, 1999

Henderson, Robert; Operating in the Courts of Heaven-Granting God the legal Right
to Fulfill His Passion and Answer Our Prayers. Robert Henderson Ministries, 2014.

ABOUT THE AUTHOR

Ebenezer B. Gyasi is the founder of Deliverance-On-The-Go Ministries geared to teaching the body of Christ to wage effective tactical spiritual warfare against demonic strongholds. Ebenezer Gyasi is an author, teacher, and cofounder of the Mountain Top Prayer Line Ministries. Ebenezer Gyasi has written the following books: Target or Weapon-Prayer Book, Killing Me Softly, Spiritual Marriage-The Curse of Illicit Sexual Union, Prayer Toolbox Volume 1, Prayer Toolbox Volume 2, Battle of The Kingdoms-End-of Year-Beginning-of-Year Forty Day Fasting and Prayer. He lives in Newark, New Jersey with his wife Nana-Yaa and Children.

Made in United States
Orlando, FL
19 July 2024

49207357R00100